KEN COO

THROUGH THE
SCHOOL
GATE

A
Teacher's
Journey

FOREWORD BY
DAVID BLUNKETT

KEN COOK CBE DL

THROUGH THE SCHOOL GATE

A Teacher's Journey

BANNISTER
PUBLICATIONS

First published in Great Britain in 2024 by
Bannister Publications Ltd
2A Market Hall, Chesterfield, Derbyshire, S40 1AR

Copyright © Ken Cook 2024

ISBN: 978-1-916823-21-1

Typeset by Bannister Publications Ltd

Printed and bound by CMP UK Ltd, in Great Britain

This book was self-published by Bannister Publications.
For more information on self-publishing visit:
www.bannisterpublications.com

CONTENTS

FOREWORD

BY LORD DAVID BLUNKETT

Ken Cook's book is about a journey. A journey which took him from newly qualified teacher through to headship, and the establishment of the South Yorkshire Leadership Centre based at Sheffield Hallam University – which I had the privilege of opening as Secretary of State for Education and Employment.

Ken was formerly the Head of Meadowhead School, which combined the original Jordanthorpe and Rowlinson schools (Ken had worked in those early years to transform the reputation of Jordanthorpe). Before Ken left the Headship, I was, as the opposition spokesman for Education, able to join the celebration of its designation as "excellent". In addition to its academic success, it also pioneered inclusion when autism was little understood and provision virtually non-existent.

I will be forever grateful to Ken for taking on, at short notice, the leadership of what was Earl Marshal School, now Fir Vale, which was on the edge of closure as parents voted with their feet against a school which had to be either transformed or closed.

In its new guise, Fir Vale has flourished, has played its part at the centre of a vibrant, multi-ethnic community, and more than justified the decision to offer a fresh start all those years ago.

In encapsulating his journey, Ken has described why teaching is such a wonderful profession: the uplifting experience of turning round the lives of youngsters, offering the opportunity to develop and use their talent, and open up a window on the world.

I'm very pleased that Ken chose to follow his wife to my city of Sheffield, and to provide a lasting legacy of which he can be justly proud.

Lord David Blunkett

St. Clement Danes
Early Influences

I am often surprised by the number of adults who recall experiences from their school days that had a profound impact on their later lives. For some it was the acquisition of knowledge that led to a lifetime of interest in a particular subject. For others it was the experience of taking part in other activities such as sport, music or drama. Others, of course, recall negative experiences that blighted their lives through to adulthood. Whatever the recollection it would almost certainly include references to teachers, many of whom shared a love of a particular subject or activity.

I was a pupil at St. Clement Danes School in London and it was there that the foundation was laid that influenced my decision to become a teacher. To be truthful, I was not academically gifted and had it not been for the inspiration of Rab Butler, who introduced the 1944 Education Act, I would have probably attended an elementary school until I reached the age of 15. There is no doubt that the key incentive for the Education Act was the approaching end of Second World War. Our Nation was emerging from a conflict in which all citizens, irrespective of class, had made great sacrifices. As the final victory approached, our national leaders were united in wanting to create a new society that recognised the contribution to the war effort of all sections of the community regardless of social class.

The 1944 Act changed the structure of secondary education in Britain and anticipated the greater opportunities for the children of the working class. The Act required each Local Authority to draw up plans to introduce secondary education for all. Although the Act did not specify how this should be achieved, many local authorities chose to prepare plans to implement what later became known as the tripartite system of grammar, technical and secondary modern schools. The method of selection was the performance in the 11+ test at the end of primary education. In reality, this was a pass-or-fail test. If you passed, you were eligible for a place in a selective school, but if you failed, you were allocated a place in a secondary modern school. It was at this time that the school leaving age was also raised to 15, which meant that those pupils attending a secondary modern school were released to join the labour market at this age. For those attending a selective school, there was a clear expectation that they would remain in school at least until they reached 16, having taken the School Certificate or, later, the General Certificate of Education (GCE). This qualification was the staging point en route to further academic or vocational qualifications.

The changes introduced by the 1944 Act were generally welcomed. They gave some working-class children an opportunity to gain qualifications and, consequently, access to more rewarding jobs. On the other hand, it was still evident that there was a greater likelihood of middle-class pupils succeeding in the 11+ tests. This led to serious questions about the validity of the 'fixed pool of ability' concept, with the attendant 'glass ceiling' through which only a minority of working-class pupils could pass.

I suppose that I was one of this minority. I came from a working class family and lived with my Mum and Dad and two older brothers in a council flat in Shepherds Bush. My brothers were quite bright and they both passed the 11+ and gained places at St. Clement Danes Grammar School. Sadly, my performance at 11+ was less illustrious and I was fortunate that the persistence of my parents and the good school reputations of my brothers encouraged the Head teacher to grant me a place.

When I started at the grammar school, I entered with an adventurous spirit but a lack of a work ethic. I made the mistake of thinking that life would continue very much the same as it was at my primary school. I soon became involved in school activities, clubs and societies. Certainly, for the first two years I made little effort with my school work and my critical school reports failed to motivate me although, they often led to serious conversations with my parents. The real problem was that I failed to realise that whilst I was enjoying the social life with my friends, they were working much more diligently at their schoolwork and homework. Matters came to a head just before the summer holiday. My Dad had completed an emergency teacher training course and was teaching at a secondary modern school. He was on holiday during the summer break and, predictably, for the next six weeks my social life was non-existent, and my studying was strictly timetabled! However, at the end of this period I had developed a new confidence and a pleasure in achieving. At the end of the following term, my report was quite different. We were tested and placed in rank order in every subject and these results were amalgamated to indicate an overall class position. Although I didn't quite reach the top of the class, I was second! From that moment, I realised that my destiny was in my own hands and that there was much more pleasure in receiving praise rather than criticism. Fortunately, my teachers positively encouraged what is referred to currently as 'soft skills' such as resilience, independence, problem-solving, self-reliance, and adventurous spirit. One of my teachers,

Bernard McCarthy, introduced a group of us to cycling and youth hostelling. As a result, I spent most of my holidays on cycling expeditions all over the country. As Londoners, mainly from working-class backgrounds, there were few opportunities to escape from the very busy capital to enjoy the pleasures of the open road. Youth hostelling gave us the opportunity to meet with people from other parts of the country and abroad. We were often away for weeks at a time and the stories of our adventures were legendary. However, the trip to France in 1956 is the freshest in my mind.

With two friends, Roy Strange and Chris Parrott, we decided to cycle to Paris. I worked at a local factory making biscuits in order to raise the money for the trip. At the time, there was a limitation on the amount of foreign currency you could take out of the country so we booked the ferry from Dover to Boulogne and a couple of youth hostels ahead of departure. Fortunately, one of my friends had a tent that we could use most of the time. Early one morning we set off from London to cycle to Dover. It took longer than we had estimated and by evening we had only reached Canterbury. We agreed that it would be wise to find a suitable place to camp for the night and to complete the journey to the ferry the next morning. Eventually, we found a wooded area close to the road and we called at the local farmhouse to ask if we could pitch our tent for the night. Permission was granted and we set up camp. When we opened the tent the next morning, we had a pleasant surprise. The farmer's wife had left some milk, bread and eggs for our breakfast! After eating and a cursory wash in an adjacent stream we went to thank the farmer and his wife before continuing to the ferry port. In the conversation they explained that they had lost their son during the Normandy landings and that our adventurous spirit reminded them of him. Eventually, we arrived at Dover and boarded the ferry. Today, most young people have some experience of travelling abroad. For us, it was a step into the unknown. I recall seeing the Cliffs of Dover fading into the distance and recalled hearing interviews with returning servicemen speaking with great emotion about the feeling of safety that they felt as they returned at the end of the war.

We arrived in Boulogne in the early evening and quickly found the youth hostel where we planned to stay the night. It was a night that changed my view of the world. Until now, I had always been a little Englander, but suddenly, I became an internationalist. The other hostellers were from all over Europe and beyond, mainly from Scandinavia but some from Australia and New Zealand. Our conversations continued long into the night and I remember our disappointment as we departed the next morning. Fortunately, we were destined to meet some of our new friends later as we journeyed to Paris, where we arrived two days later. We spent our first night at the youth hostel close to the Gare du Nord railway station before moving to a campsite in the Bois de Boulogne. The next few days were full of exciting discoveries. We climbed the Eiffel Tower, walked along the Champs Elysee, viewed the tomb of the unknown soldier at the Arc de Triomphe, took a trip on the River Seine and visited many other famous sites. Many young people today who have experienced holidays in more exotic places might consider our experience as very ordinary. To us, we were pioneering after a devastating war where our only impressions of Paris were formed by cinema newsreels showing foreign soldiers in occupation.

After a week we started our journey back, camping near Amiens and Montreux before arriving at the ferry port in the afternoon. We planned to spend the last night of our trip in the Youth Hostel in Canterbury, but the ferry was late arriving in Dover, which meant that it was not possible to reach the hostel on time. We made the decision to cycle directly back to London. Soon it was time to split up to take the final part of the journey back to our homes. In the very early hours of the morning, I arrived at my house to wake up my parents and to face the admonishment of my Mother, who had spent three weeks wondering where I was and whether I was safe. However, after eating a hearty breakfast, followed by giving a full account of my adventures, everything returned to normal and I prepared to return to school to enter the sixth form.

The independence that was encouraged in my early days in Secondary School was a valuable asset with the greater freedom but higher expectations of being in the sixth form. It soon became apparent that the enjoyment of adventure that I had experienced now needed to be accompanied by a greater level of commitment to my studies. By now I had already made up my mind that I wanted to follow the example of my teachers and to help other young people to develop an independence of spirit with a determination to follow their dreams. It was clear that I wanted to be a teacher! I wanted to introduce others to a world where anything was possible if you had the courage to reach for it. It was not such a difficult challenge. I was a pupil at my school for the greater part of the 1950s. This was a period of great national optimism which, almost certainly, influenced everyone who was fortunate to be alive at this time. The war had ended, and the new Elizabethan Age was heralded. I remember the national pride on Coronation Day when it was announced that Everest had been conquered. The whole school was taken to the Savoy cinema in East Acton to see the film that had been made during the ascent.

Not everything was positive though. The England football team was beaten for the first time at Wembley by a brilliant Hungarian side. At this time, England always played on a Wednesday afternoon and my support for the national team caused me to truant from school. I cycled to Wembley and locked my bike to a railing outside the ground. As I recall, we lost 6:3. My disappointment was compounded the next morning when I had to face my Head Teacher to be inflicted with both emotional and physical pain. Many years later, when I was the Director of the Leadership Centre at Sheffield Hallam University, I spent some time in Budapest on behalf of the British Council. I told a group of education leaders of the painful consequence of watching Hungary beat England. At the end of the day, the group took me from the university to the People's Stadium where, the following year, Hungary beat England 7:1. I often reflect on my decision to go to Wembley and the reaction I received from the deputy head teacher who was also my mathematics teacher. It was his lesson that I had skipped. His words are still in my memory, "You have only one bite of the cherry, Cook, and yesterday you missed an important lesson on the use of log tables." How I would love to meet him now to tell him that I can't recall any occasion after leaving school when I used log tables but I could still name every one of the 22 players on the pitch at Wembley on that Wednesday afternoon!

One other event I remember from my school days was an encounter with a national hero. The Hammersmith Hospital was next door to my school. There was a gate from our playing field into the hospital grounds. I was playing football on the field and clashed with a fellow team player and received a cut above the eyebrow that needed stitching. I was taken through the gate into the hospital, where a white-coated doctor arrived to insert the stitches. The doctor was Roger Bannister, the first man to run a mile in under four minutes. I spent the next few days enjoying the reflected glory that I received from my classmates.

As my time at school was rapidly approaching completion, I had to take my preparations for 'A' level examinations more seriously. My Dad, who had suffered long periods of unemployment before the war, was adamant that I should get a job with a pension so teaching was an acceptable option in his eyes. He wanted me to emulate my older brother, who was the first one in the immediate and extended family to attend university, so I applied for a place at the London School of Economics. I obviously did not impress the interview panel and I received a rejection letter even before the 'A' level results were posted. During the summer holiday, I found a job working for a publishing company. It was a small company publishing paperback novels. I enjoyed working with the other people and became friendly with the sales manager. It was the custom to target publicity in the local area from which an author came, so at weekends I would accompany the sales manager to different parts of the country to put up displays in local bookshops. On one of these trips the manager told me of his plans to leave the company and to set up his own enterprise, publishing short stories. He asked me to join him and I was very tempted. However, my wise Dad dissuaded me by reminding of my desire to be a teacher. At the time though it was too late to pursue a university place but I found the City of Leicester Teacher Training College had some places available. I was called for an interview and I was offered an immediate start.

The College was in a period of transition from being a Women's College to becoming mixed. I was probably in the second tranche of men admissions. I soon made friends, some with whom I am still in contact. It was a happy time. There was such a shortage of teachers that students were almost certain to achieve qualification. The academic demands were reasonable, and there was a spirit of camaraderie in helping each other when our subject knowledge was weak. It was more competitive, however, when it came to the practice of teaching. For those of us training to teach in secondary schools, we gained immense kudos from undertaking successful teaching practices in tough inner city secondary modern schools. I think our education lecturers must have spent long hours debating which schools would be best for each of us for our final teaching practice. I ended up at Campbell Square School in the centre of Northampton, which meant that I had to live in a boarding house during the week, but I could return to Leicester each weekend. Although Campbell Square was a tough Boys'

School with many challenging adolescents, I really enjoyed my time there. I was with another student who was a good footballer. He had represented Great Britain in the Olympics and he was also on the books of Millwall FC. His presence encouraged the staff to organise a staff v. pupils football match. My fellow student, Richie Ward, was outstanding, and I was able to glow under his shadow. We had earned our stripes in the eyes of the pupils and were granted a level of respect that was not customary for student teachers. When returning to college, we had stories to tell, and one other student seemed to enjoy listening to me. She was training to be a teacher of infants and she was a year ahead of me. She was from Sheffield, and when I told one of my brothers about her, he was aghast. My family were typical southerners who viewed the North as another country. I must confess that before I met Jennifer I thought that as well. Eventually, she returned to Sheffield, and I had to remain in Leicester for another year. I managed an occasional weekend to travel north to see her and to meet her family, who always made me feel welcome, although my first meeting with Jennifer's Dad was intimidating. He was in a local hospital after having an operation to reconnect a detached retina. At this time, this was quite a complicated procedure. I remember entering the hospital ward with Jennifer to be scrutinised by about twelve male patients all lying in bed wondering who this young man had come to visit.

Eventually, I spied a patient whose eyes were heavily bandaged. As we approached him, Jennifer made the formal introduction. I soon realised how difficult it was to engage in a conversation with a stranger who was unable to see me! I never knew what his first impression of me was, but over the following months, I realised he was a kindred spirit. He was an engineer who was used to solving problems, and he encouraged my belief that you should always strive to overcome barriers.

As I approached the final weeks of my training, it became clear that I had to make a decision. Either London or Sheffield. After some deliberation, my spirit of adventure and, of course, the girl led me to apply for a teaching post in Sheffield. A few days after attending an interview at the Education Offices, I received a letter telling me of my appointment at Coleridge Road Secondary Modern Boys School in the east end of Sheffield. The east end was the industrial part of the city occupied by steelworks and other factories.

MY INTRODUCTION TO SHEFFIELD

COLERIDGE ROAD SECONDARY MODERN BOYS' SCHOOL

I arrived at Sheffield Midland Station in June 1961. It was planned that I would spend a few days with Jennifer's family to allow me time to familiarise myself with the city and to seek suitable accommodation. It was a Saturday, so Jennifer was able to meet me at the station. Although I had visited Sheffield previously, the walk from the station, up a steep hill to the city centre, was unfamiliar. The haze of smoke from factory chimneys partially blocked the sunshine. The stone-built buildings were discoloured by many years of this smoke. To be truthful, it was not a good introduction to the city where I was destined to spend the rest of my life. Things improved when I was greeted by Jennifer's family. Her Mother, who was originally from Liverpool, had prepared a meal, and after a pleasant evening with the family, which I suspect was my interview for them to judge my suitability as a partner for their daughter, I took myself to bed.

The next morning, I had a short telephone conversation with my own parents, who were clearly disappointed that I was not returning to London. They had the view, prevalent to this day amongst many southerners, that people choosing to live in Sheffield must be suffering from a serious mental condition. How wrong they were! Over the next few days I had to consider the actions I needed to take before I was to start teaching in the following September at Coleridge Road School. There were two priorities. The first was to find somewhere to live and the second was to find a temporary job. Within a few days, I found a bedsit at a very reasonable rent. The room was part of an old detached house in the district of Sharrow. The proximity to a bus route leading to the City Centre made it an ideal location. The owners of the house were an older couple whose children had flown the nest to live in other parts of the country some years earlier. They soon made me feel at home.

Having found excellent accommodation I had the immediate problem of finding the funds to pay the rent. At this time, it was quite easy for students to find temporary jobs in their vacations, and after a brief search through the Sheffield Star, the local newspaper, I found an advert seeking a machine operator at Laycock Engineering located in the Abbeydale area of the City. A quick 'phone call followed by a short interview resulted in the offer of an immediate start, working on the production line making overdrives for Volvo cars. Fortunately, Jennifer was able to find a discarded set of overalls that belonged to her Dad and the next morning I reported for work at 7.30 am. My foreman was a former regular serviceman who had been well-trained in giving instructions to young recruits. By the end of my first day, I had completed my training. The next day, bright and early, I was standing at a machine with which I would become very familiar over the next eight weeks. I soon learned other important routines as well, such as clocking in and out and calling at the finance office to collect a pay packet!

Even though the pay was more than I would earn when I started teaching, I still had to plan to save enough to see me through my first month of teaching before I received my salary. Very soon, an opportunity arose when the foreman asked if I would like to change to working on the night shift. The pay was significantly better and the working hours suited me. On the night shift I only had to work four nights a week from 6.00 pm until 6.00 am the next morning. Although the hours each day were much longer it allowed me a day off each week.

Working on a production line with no understanding of the relevance of how your part of the process was important to the production of the final article reminded me, very much, of some of my lessons at school. I wrote earlier about mathematics lessons during which much time was used to teach some topics that failed to have relevance in later life. However, the monotony of the job was broken during tea and lunch breaks when I was able to enjoy banter with my fellow workers. As I got to know them, I soon appreciated the Yorkshire sense of humour. Being a southerner, I was often the butt of the jokes but, to their credit, my blunt responses were always enjoyed.

Eventually, September arrived, and on the first day of term, I set off on the bus, hoping to arrive at Coleridge Road School in good time. Finding the school presented some difficulties. I managed to arrive at the bus terminus without a problem, but I then had to change onto a different bus that would take me along Attercliffe Common in the direction of Rotherham. I was not sure of the best place to alight from the bus, so I asked the conductor to let me know when we arrived at the appropriate stop. Coming from London, I was not used to starting conversations with people on public transport, so, to my surprise, all of the nearby passengers added their advice on my best option. Although I had some difficulty in understanding the east end of Sheffield accent and vocabulary, for the first time I appreciated the warmth, sense of humour and pride of the people of the city.

When I arrived at the school, some of the pupils were playing football in the yard. When they saw me they stopped the game and one young man asked, "Are you the new teacher?" When I replied in the affirmative he said, 'well, you will be teaching my class'. He then added, "Shall I take you to the staff room?" As I entered the staff room all ten of my new colleagues were present. Some of them were ex-servicemen, and most of them had been at the school for many years. The first question I was asked was, "Where are you from lad?" My reply, "London", was greeted with the reposte, "They should push that into the ....Thames." Thus began a journey for which I will be forever grateful. Over the next few years I learned and appreciated the Yorkshire mentality and sense of humour. My preconceptions were challenged. I genuinely believed that the rivalry was between Yorkshire and Lancashire. How wrong I was. I soon realised that the rivalry was between Yorkshire and anybody else! This was particularly demonstrated when Yorkshire played cricket. In the eyes of my colleagues, every other county was a southern one, including Lancashire! Even the pupils in my first class were astonished at my reply to the question, "Which football team do you support?" My answer, "Queens Park Rangers", caused a period of silence until someone had the courage to say, "That can't be right. It's got to be Wednesday or United."

My first year of teaching took me on a steep learning curve. I began to understand the meaning of the unfamiliar words and phrases used by my pupils. The boys were very tolerant and seemed to enjoy the reversed role of teacher and pupil. At the time, the musical film 'The King and I' was popular, and the song of the Governess with the phrase, 'When you become a teacher by your pupils, you'll be taught' seemed to fit my situation. I learned new words such as 'ganzie', meaning cardigan, 'mardy' meaning disgruntled, 'jennel' meaning alleyway and encountered new statements like, 'I've finished my work to press' meaning I have completed the task and 'spotball' meaning you are picking on me. There were similar mysteries outside of school. I recall trying to buy crumpets at my local shop to be informed that in Sheffield they were known as 'pikelets'. Even at the fish and chip shop I encountered a different version of a fishcake to the one I was used to in London. To me a fishcake was a piece of fish fried between two slices of potato. In Sheffield, fish and mashed potatoes are fried together. My most notable misinterpretation occurred on a bus journey late one night on a very cold wintry night. I was alone, and the bus was almost empty, apart from a middle-aged female conductor. We struck up a conversation. She told me how glad she would be when her shift ended. In the conversation, she said she felt 'starved'. I spent the rest of the night worrying that I had been unable to offer her some sweets or chocolate. The next morning, I recounted this story to some of my colleagues, who treated the plight of this poor woman with great jocularity. Eventually, they explained that the conductor meant she was cold!

Little did I realise the impact on me of the conversations I was having with both my pupils and adults. At the end of my first year of teaching, I went back to London to visit my parents. At this time, I still thought of myself as a true Londoner. Whilst at my parent's house, the postman came to deliver the letters. I was just going out so he put the letters into my hand and we passed some pleasantries. At the end of our conversation, the postman said, "You are not from round here, are you?" I had suddenly become a foreigner in my own country!

I returned to Sheffield at the end of the holiday, ready to start my second year at Coleridge Road. I anticipated that this was going to be a good year because the mistakes made previously could be corrected. It was, in fact, a year when the judgements of me changed. No longer was it whether I could maintain a good level of discipline. It became the year when I would be judged on the quality of my teaching. I still had a class of thirty and I was still expected to teach them all subjects. The difference was that the Head Teacher and the LEA Advisers spent more time observing my teaching. The traditional academic subjects presented me with few problems but a threatened visit from the PE Adviser caused some consternation. Whilst I enjoy sport, teaching PE was never part of my training. At this time, there was a new emphasis on educational gymnastics and many of the primary schools were embracing this new concept. By good fortune, my future wife was a primary school teacher and she explained some of the thinking behind the new initiative. No longer was it acceptable for a PE lesson to stress physical exertion until exhaustion. The emphasis now was more on problem-solving and exploring different ways to perform a physical task. As I had no formal training to teach PE I used my new knowledge in my lessons.

A few weeks after starting this new regime I had a message from the Head Teacher that the PE Adviser would be in school later that day to observe my PE lesson. I must admit to facing this prospect with great trepidation. I had trained the pupils to start the lesson in good order. Each of them had a task which involved setting up the equipment in an orderly fashion. Once this was done, the class was split into groups, and each group was required to undertake a series of activities. The tasks had to involve some problem solving, typically, 'how many ways can you find to balance on two parts of your body?' or 'demonstrate four ways to traverse a beam balance'. Towards the end of the lesson, I stopped the class, and the instruction was given to put the equipment away. Once the pupils had changed, it was break time, so I was prepared for the feedback from the Adviser. This was memorable. The Adviser was full of praise for the lesson and asked me if I would do a demonstration lesson for PE teachers in other secondary schools. As many of these teachers had completed their training at Loughborough or Carnegie I realised that this was a great accolade.

I must confess, however, that my new found expertise in gymnastics did not extend to the new emphasis on team games. There was much talk amongst the so-called experts on emphasising universal attacking and defending skills. Personally, I was unable to embrace these changes. I recognised that the best way to learn these skills was by playing football, hockey or other competitive games, so I continued to support the School sports teams that were entered into inter-school competitions. We were only a small secondary school but we enjoyed success in most sports. One of my greatest pleasures was when my cricket team won the Sheffield inter-schools trophy, The Barber Shield. Seeing a silver shield engraved with Coleridge Road School attached to the trophy provided me with a double pleasure. First, I took the trophy into the staff room and said, 'It took a southerner to come here to teach you Yorkshire men to play cricket'. After receiving the expected good-humoured abuse, we all went to the hall for an assembly where the Head Teacher presented the trophy to the team. For a few days we all enjoyed the pride that some might have interpreted as smugness!

Shortly before the end of the Summer term the Head Teacher came to my classroom to tell me that he had just enrolled three new pupils and he was going to put them into my class. This was a time when there was a large influx of immigrants, mainly from Pakistan. This was indeed a problem. As a secondary trained teacher I had little skill to teach reading. However, over the holiday I took advice from Jennifer. She was trained to teach reading to much younger pupils but the reading schemes that were designed for younger pupils were not appropriate for older pupils who could not speak English. To compound the problem, when I returned to School after the holiday I found that a further nine pupils were to be enrolled, making my class total forty-two. My colleagues recognised that as these pupils, and possibly, others progressed that this was now a whole school issue and it was essential to develop a strategy that recognised the needs of our new pupils. We finally decided on a course of action. As there was no immediate hope of additional resources being provided by the LEA and there were no suitable teaching resources for older, non-English speaking pupils, we agreed on a long-term strategy. First, we decided that the best way to learn a new language would be to speak it at all times. Later in my teaching career, when considering the teaching of a foreign language, my skilled language teachers always emphasised the importance of consistently using the target language in lessons. Secondly, it would be necessary to introduce additional lessons focusing on reading and speaking skills specifically for this group of pupils. Finally, we agreed to find a way to introduce one-to-one support from others familiar with the target language, in this case, English. The only problem was, of course, that the additional resources and support would not be available immediately. However, I was about to learn something about my pupils that influenced my thinking for the rest of my career. I shared the dilemma with my class who, by this time, had fully accepted the newcomers and involved them in their playground games and activities. They soon volunteered to act as reading mentors. Whilst this was not an ideal solution, it certainly led to improvements in reading and the positive and unexpected outcome of the forging of some strong friendships.

Many people might think that being assigned to teach in the industrial part of Sheffield, in a Victorian building surrounded by smoke emitting factory chimneys, with pupils from homes, often with shared outside toilets, would be less than desirable. How wrong they would be. I often hear people from more advantaged backgrounds talking about how well they have achieved in life's competitions. Many had the advantage of parents who could pull strings and provide experiences that were beyond the comprehension of the children and families living in this deprived community. Success for some emphasised failure for others. But the pupils at Coleridge Road were not failures. They and their families suffered disadvantage but they wouldn't inflict disadvantage on their neighbours. They were proud and honest. They respected those who respected them.

As a mere southerner, I was pondering how I could become accepted as an adopted Yorkshire man when I heard the pupils talking about 'The General'. It was the custom that all pupils had nicknames but this one was unfamiliar. When I asked my class who the General was, they replied, "That's what we call you." When asked, "Why?" the leader of the group explained, "Well, your name is Cook. We all know about Captain Cook, but we think you're better than that." Sadly, I think my new passport has been lost in the post!

Norfolk School

For both Jennifer and myself, those early days of teaching were demanding. We were making our way in our chosen careers and there was little time for a social life. As young teachers, our salaries were not great, but one summer holiday we managed to save enough money to pay for a 10-day break to Switzerland. The cost of the holiday was £29.00 each. We travelled with two friends who had been married for a year. After a long two-day coach journey from Ostend, we arrived at the Hotel Rigiblick on Lake Lucerne, and we spent the next week taking excursions to see the beautiful scenery. It was such a pleasure to enjoy our evening meals on the patio, watching the sun go down over the lake. It must have been the ambience of these moments that led Jennifer and I to decide that we would plan to marry in the following August.

When we returned from an idyllic summer holiday we were soon back in our working routine in our respective schools, but now with additional tasks of planning a wedding and deciding where we would live. By this time, I had become committed to Sheffield, and Jennifer wanted to continue teaching at her school, so the first decision was clear. The next issue was to find suitable accommodation. One thing we agreed on was that we didn't want to pay rent on a property so we explored opportunities to purchase. Sadly, our earnings did not warrant a sufficient mortgage to purchase a suitable property in Sheffield. By this time we had become friendly with another couple who were facing the same predicament as us. One Sunday, they suggested that we should take a short trip to Dronfield, a town in Derbyshire adjacent to the Sheffield border where a local builder was planning to build a large new estate. The houses were to be detached and semi-detached three-bedroom properties. After checking that there was a regular bus service that went to the centre of Sheffield, we decided to put a non-returnable deposit of £25.00 on an, as yet, unbuilt house that would eventually cost £2400.00. After a number of rejections, we managed to get a 25-year mortgage with repayments set at the equivalent of £11.50 per month.

Whilst I often joke about the Yorkshire sense of humour and their view of southerners, it was at this time that I discovered the true generosity of the Yorkshire spirit. I realised that moving to a new house would require practical skills that I did not possess nor the tools I would need when I acquired these skills. However, as the time approached to move into the new house, a colleague at Coleridge Road who was a teacher of woodwork gave me a large box of old tools, some of which I still have and use. Other colleagues advised me on how to prepare a garden from a building site, and my father-in-law gave me an old Ford Thames van and supervised my driving lessons.

It was a very happy time but, inevitably, there was a cloud on the horizon. The Head Teacher took me aside one day to tell me that the Authority was planning to close Coleridge Road School. He continued to tell me that another school was seeking a teacher to be responsible for the library. The post had a responsibility allowance. The Head's advice was to take this opportunity before decisions would be made by the Authority that were not within my control.

I was eventually appointed to this new post, where I had a full teaching timetable but with the additional responsibility of setting up a new library in another part of the building. I was also a form teacher and remember, with gratitude, the help that my pupils provided by staying behind after school to move the books and shelves to the new site. However, there was a distinct difference in the atmosphere of my new school compared to Coleridge Road. Most of the pupils lived on two housing estates, The Manor and Arbourthorne. Their families had been moved to these estates when the Council decided to clear some of the old terraced properties in the industrial areas of Sheffield. Unlike the families that still lived around Coleridge Road, these pupils lived on estates with little or no community cohesion. In this situation, the role of the school was critical and, credit due to some of the teachers, they saw their responsibilities as much greater than of classroom teaching. The development of a school spirit was addressed, mainly, by an emphasis on sport. There were school teams in football, hockey, netball, athletics etc. I soon realised that I needed to become involved. Just after I joined the school, the teacher responsible for the cross-country team was to be seconded for a year to undertake in-service training as a teacher of special needs. He not only organised the school team but he was also the Secretary of the Sheffield Schools' Cross Country League. Very soon, he approached me to ask if I would take on his responsibilities until he was to return the following year. I willingly accepted both the responsibility for the school team and the wider challenge of being the Secretary of the League. This meant that on many Saturday mornings, I would meet my pupils at the school gate and guide them, generally on a bus, to another school, often across the city.

On one of these occasions at the race venue at Hinde

House School, I had two visitors. One was John Phillips, who had been a mentor to me at Coleridge Road. I had learned so much from this wonderful Welshman who was revered by all who came into contact with him. When Coleridge Road closed, the pupils were transferred to Park House School, and John was appointed as the deputy head. On this morning he was accompanied by another gentleman. As we walked around the cross-country course, John introduced me to Mr Aizlewood, who was the Head Teacher at Park House. After some polite conversation, John informed me that there was a Head of Department post to be advertised at the school. Very discreetly, it was suggested that I might be interested in applying.

I must admit that the thought of returning to the East End of Sheffield to teach pupils with whom I was familiar filled me with joy. When I arrived home, I told Jennifer about this opportunity, only to receive information that gave me another incentive to apply. She told me that she was in the early stages of pregnancy, which meant that she would have to make plans to stop work. This was, therefore, an additional factor to reinforce my decision to apply for the post.

As soon as the post was advertised, I sent for an application form which required the names of two referees, one of whom should be my current Head Teacher. One morning, I arrived at school earlier than usual to find that the Head Teacher was already at his desk. This was the right time to face the music, so I knocked on his study door and was invited to enter. Incoherently, I told the Head of the impending addition to my family, which meant that I needed to seek more responsibility so that my salary would increase to partly cover the loss of my wife's income. His reply was short, "I thought it wouldn't be long." Eventually, after the interviews which involved two other candidates, I was offered the appointment at Park House starting in the following September.

Park House School
New Responsibilities

The summer holiday before I started at Park House was very busy. Preparation for the impending addition to the family was both exciting and costly. I realised that once I started my new job there would be little time available, so I was determined to use the few weeks of the holiday to completely decorate the house, including preparing a bedroom as a nursery. Fortunately, there was help available from family and friends who not only provided physical help but also items required by a new born baby. By the beginning of September, I was ready to start at my new school, while Jennifer started her maternity preparations for the birth of our daughter, Anna, in November.

Early on the first day of term I set off in my old, temperamental Ford Thames Van to arrive at school in good time. The day started with a short staff meeting at which the Head Teacher introduced me to the staff. I was probably feeling sensitive because I was insecure but I detected a lack of enthusiasm amongst some of the staff, two of whom were members of my department. The rest of that week was very busy with meeting individual teachers and greeting the pupils in the classes I was to teach. I was embarking on my first management responsibility and I was anxious to earn the respect of the members of my department.

Over the years, I have discerned that good leadership is not something you can learn from a textbook. Of course, there are techniques that you can be taught but the most effective leaders I have met always say that their main influence was observing other outstanding leaders. At this time, the main influence on me was John Phillips, who, at Coleridge Road, had demonstrated the 'soft skills' of encouragement, determination, respect, appreciation and selflessness to which I now aspired. John was now the Deputy Head teacher at Park House. I can only conclude that good leadership is something you can learn by observation and emulation, but you can't be taught.

During the early days of my time in post, I became aware that there were wide variations in the professional standards of the teachers in my department. Some would have been a credit in any school but others (two in number!) seemed totally unconcerned about lesson preparation or meaningful assessment that would lead to improved pupil performance. There was clearly an urgent need for intervention. My starting point was to take time to observe the teaching practices of the teachers. Most of them welcomed this review, but I soon encountered resistance from the two teachers, whom I identified almost immediately upon my arrival. One of them was responsible for the delivery of library based lessons in which the pupils were meant to be able to research topics that occurred in history, geography or civics lessons. I made several visits to the library only to find that it was the practice of the teacher to allow the pupils a very short time to select a book and then to sit in silence for the rest of the lesson, reading or making notes. The presence of a cane on the teacher's desk indicated strict obedience was enforced. Today, of course, corporal punishment is outlawed but at this time, in some schools, teachers were allowed to employ this sanction. I made it clear that this practice was inappropriate and that the cane should be removed immediately. I also insisted that the teacher should prepare weekly lesson notes for my approval that reflected a focus on the curriculum being taught by his departmental colleagues. Suddenly, he was made to realise that he was now part of a team, and his deliberate attempts to remain isolated and unaccountable were not in the interests of the pupils or his colleagues. By the end of that year, the teacher in question realised that, despite his bluster, he was losing face in the eyes of the other staff and his only option was to resign. My advice to all young teachers is to understand that schools don't exist for the benefit of the teachers and that all possible actions should be based on what is in the interests of the pupils. We were now entering a period when the effectiveness of the teacher was not just about classroom control but also about the quality and relevance of the teaching.

The other difficult teacher in my department was a well-qualified history graduate who had the potential to make a substantial contribution. Although he was associated with the dissidents, he clearly wanted to contribute to the department. Over a period of time he became a valuable asset to departmental discussions, and he, together with others, embraced the idea of experimenting with team teaching. This involved each member of the department taking responsibility for preparing and delivering a key lesson to the whole year group. This would be followed by individual class lessons delivered by the other teachers using worksheets and guidance notes prepared by the leader. At the end of the year, we all agreed that the organisation of this experiment was too much of a burden, so we abandoned any future development of the project. However, it was not a disaster. We developed a unified assessment policy that we continued to use in subsequent years, and we started to discuss task differentiation in a mixed-ability class. We were now a team with agreed objectives and a strategic plan.

After a short period, I was able to engage with other staff in wider school activities. The school leaving age was still 15, so the teachers were not constrained by the need to prepare the pupils for external examinations. Indeed, few of the staff had ever experienced this responsibility, although this was about to change. We were entering a time when there was concern about our national ability to compete in the ever more important global economy, which was becoming increasingly competitive, knowledge-based and profit-driven. Discussions at the national level indicated that all schools should begin to focus on our need to contribute to the national economic performance by preparing our pupils for progression to achieving higher level skills.

It was an interesting time and, on reflection, I think many teachers were resistant to the changes that were about to come. I realised that I needed to have a better understanding of the new direction, so I enrolled on a two-year evening course at the Sheffield Polytechnic (later to become Sheffield Hallam University) to gain a diploma in Education Management. The focus of the course was to explore the need for, and the implementation of, a transformed learning culture which would equip young people for work. As a result of this emphasis the climate in schools was changing from one where teachers were in control of the curriculum to a new era of a prescriptive, externally imposed curriculum that made teachers more accountable. Predictably, teachers and their union leaders opposed change and a period of teacher strikes followed.

At Park House, the Head Teacher embraced the necessary change of culture, and he asked me to take on the role of Head of Upper School. My new position included responsibility for careers education and the preparation for the raising of the school leaving age to 16. Until this point, the school had been part of a limited Sheffield LEA experiment and was called a high school. This meant that pupils in Y8 were given the option to transfer to Hinde House School on the assumption that they would stay on until they were 16 and take external examinations. Not many of our pupils took this option but those that did were generally the more able. The remaining pupils at Park House were expected to leave at 15. However, two years before ROSLA we decided to offer the remaining pupils the possibility to stay on for another year and to be prepared for external examinations. Eventually, the parents of twenty pupils agreed for their children to join the first examination group.

We were only able to offer a restricted number of GCE/CSE subjects. English and mathematics were obviously a priority, but teachers of woodwork, metalwork, textiles and civics were keen to take part. The timetable was arranged so that one day of the week was clear for other activities. After some discussions with the Sheffield Further Education Colleges, who, at this time, were still part of the Sheffield LEA, I was able to negotiate with them Link courses, which involved one-year vocational courses requiring attendance on one day each week in secretarial studies, electronics, engineering and building studies. It was agreed that those pupils who completed one of these options could progress onto an appropriate FE course regardless of their final examination grades.

Within a year we had achieved several breakthroughs. First the teachers had gained knowledge of preparing pupils for external assessment. Second, the parents and pupils realised that there was a route to gaining higher level qualifications via the relationship established with the FE Colleges.

The following year we also became a partner with the neighbouring Hinde House School to encourage those pupils who wanted to follow traditional sixth form studies. In order to establish this as a natural choice for Park House pupils I spent an afternoon each week teaching in the sixth form at Hinde House. This was to have a major impact on my own future career!

Park House School
Projects

Fortunately, the demands on the teachers to implement these changes did not diminish the commitment of the Park House School staff to encouraging self-reliance and problem-solving. One particular teacher, Dave Cliffe, had led an adventurous life including racing his Mini Cooper car at many of our national race tracks. The stories of his hair-raising experiences were legendary in the staff room. One day, he arrived at School to inform some of the like-minded teachers that he had discovered an ex-War Department fire engine gathering dust at the now-defunct Rotherham Fire Service Depot. Although it had been registered in 1938 it had only 3000 miles on the clock. He explained that the vehicle was to be sold at a knockdown price, but the conversion for it to carry passengers would need some investment. His request for help was unanimously agreed, and a series of fundraising events were planned. Some of the senior pupils, helped by teachers, set about organising the usual fund raising activities such as sponsored walks and raffles. They organised a wool collection of old woollen clothing that could be sold for recycling. For a month, every assembly opened with a group of pupils who had formed a singing group called the 'Woolley Jumpers' delivering their own compositions, encouraging other pupils to get their families to contribute. As soon as we reached the financial target the conversion began. Pupils in the woodwork shop made wooden panels, others in the metalwork shop fabricated the metal side panels whilst the cushions were prepared in the needlework room. Of course, these activities were supervised by teachers, but the pupils were involved throughout the actual construction and planning. Within a short period of time, the bus passed a roadworthy inspection and was available for use.

My first experience of driving the vehicle came when I took a group of pupils for a residential few days to a place called Unstone Grange. This was an old mansion in North Derbyshire with extensive grounds and outbuildings. This was the first visit of many. The purpose was to give a group of youngsters from fairly deprived backgrounds the experience of learning in a more relaxed situation. Colleagues from school would come out to the Grange to organise half-day sessions in surveying, nature walks, art, and drama. The pupils also visited the local farm where they experienced animal husbandry. In the evenings, we had a formal meal and entertained visitors in the lounge. At the end of the evening, we would have a barbeque in a nearby field under a starlit sky. It was not unusual that on the morning of our return after a week away, I found some pupils in tears because this had been a very special experience, and they were treated and respected as individuals whose contributions to the group were valued.

The bus became a central feature of so many other activities. It was used to take sports teams to other schools and it was used on many foreign visits, two of which I recall with fond memories. I was responsible for the careers education programme which meant I often met with employers, especially when arranging works visits and work experience for the older pupils. We were always concerned about making these visits affordable for all pupils, so I was delighted when an exciting opportunity arose for our first visit to Germany, offered by one of our partners, the Recruitment Officer from the Sheffield Army Careers Office. One day, he contacted me to inform me that there was an opportunity to take a group to visit the Royal Engineers Regiment based in Hamelin in Germany. I briefly consulted with Dave Cliffe who immediately jumped at the idea and started preparations for the first visit of many in the bus. By the start of the summer holiday, everything was ready for departure. 20 boys and 3 teachers left the school to drive to the ferry at Calais, where we arrived in the late evening. We set off to drive to Hamelin, passing through Brussels. As it was very late, we stopped at a service area surrounded by a forest. In no time, Dave produced a large groundsheet that we laid out in a secluded part of the forest, and we all slept soundly for 3/4 hours. As daylight broke, we woke and enjoyed some tea in plastic cups. We were soon continuing our journey over the German border, heading to our destination.

We arrived at the barracks in Hamelin in the early afternoon to be greeted by the commanding officer who outlined the plan for the week. Eventually, the boys were taken by two NCO's to the nearby dormitories where they would be sleeping. In the evening, the teachers had an evening meal with the officers and teachers from the school set up for the children of the soldiers' families whilst the boys ate in the mess, where they were pleased to meet several soldiers from Yorkshire.

The next few days were spent on exciting activities like driving a tank and going to the shooting range, but one activity made a big impact on me. One night, we were informed that we were going on a night build. I should be clear that our hosts were the Amphibious Engineers Regiment who were always in the forefront of a battle responsible for constructing pontoons for the following tanks and vehicles to cross the river. Hamelin is situated on the River Weser, a very fast-flowing river. That night, young army recruits were tasked to build a bridge over the wide and wild river. These young soldiers were only a little older than our pupils. With great skill, they manoeuvred large sections into position, showing an amazing level of teamwork and responsibility. It was great credit to the Army that a group of young men, probably from deprived backgrounds, had received a level of training that gave them confidence in their skills and in their comrades.

On the day before we were due to depart from Hamelin the Commanding Officer organised our final visit. We travelled in the back of an army lorry to visit the concentration camp at Belsen. The boys had only a sketchy knowledge of the significance of the camp, so the soldier driver of the lorry gave a brief explanation of what they would find. The camp was surrounded by woods and there was a wooded area inside the walls. The soldier explained that whilst we could hear the bird song outside the wall there would be silence on the inside. Either by chance or fact, this proved to be true. Inside the camp, there were mounds with very large numbers written on the side. The boys, some of whom I taught civics (government and politics), were shocked when they realised that these were the graves of the people who died in the camp. I had spent many lessons discussing the meaning of democracy and the importance of 'eternal vigilance'. This visit meant no further explanations were necessary.

Our second visit overseas in the following August also involved travelling to Germany. This time, however, it was a trip to Sheffield's Twin City of Bochum. The twinning arrangement was agreed in 1950 to create opportunities for civic, economic and academic exchanges. At the time of our visit, there had been little opportunity for school visits, so we saw this visit as a chance to be pioneers and to represent our city at the highest level. One of the greatest virtues of many of the young people who were born and lived in the east end of Sheffield was the intense loyalty that they showed to their schools, their teachers, their fellow pupils and, of course, to their favourite football team. As we followed the same arrangements as the previous year on our journey to Dover, I took the opportunity to stress the importance of this visit. Not only our school but our city would be under scrutiny.

Eventually, we arrived at the ferry port and continued across the Channel to Calais. The journey to Bochum followed the same pattern as the previous year and we had a long stop at a service station en route. The service station had a café and the pupils and staff were able to enjoy a welcome breakfast. After a while, I realised that Dave had disappeared. He had decided to return to the bus to make some mechanical checks and he found a watering can that he could use to top up the radiator with water. We returned to the bus just as he was having a conversation with a man in an official uniform. The conversation that followed was very amusing. The man in uniform said to Dave, "Haus gun." Dave, like the rest of us, had little knowledge of German and after a second 'haus gun' from the official, he responded, "Me English, me no speak German", to which the official replied, "I'm......................... English. Has your hose gone?'" It turned out that the official was, in fact, a uniformed English coach driver taking a party of tourists on holiday.

When we arrived in Bochum we soon found the Rathaus (Town Hall) and we received a warm welcome from the Oberburgermeister (Mayor) and other officials before departing to the hostel where we would be staying during our visit. The rest of that day was spent settling in and preparing for an official welcome and lunch the next day. I had instructed the pupils to bring their school blazers and ties ready for this occasion.

We were not the only visitors. A group of Ghanaian university students were also at the welcome lunch. Perhaps it was because our pupils were wearing their school uniforms or because they were worried not to make a mistake the officials thought they were from a more socially advantaged part of Sheffield than the reality. At the end of the meal, the Mayor gave a welcoming speech to all the visitors and invited the group from Ghana to sing one of their national songs. The quality of the singing was magnificent. I enjoyed listening to them until the Mayor announced, "Now the visitors from Sheffield will sing" We were completely wrong-footed, but on the journey to Bochum, we had occupied ourselves by singing songs that were familiar, one of which was 'On Ilkley Moor Baht at'. As the impromptu choir gathered, I told them to sing with gusto. I announced to the audience that we had chosen to sing a traditional peasant song from our own County of Yorkshire. I can report that the pupils did not let us down and they were heartily clapped when the song finished.

The rest of our time in Bochum included a visit to a school and the Aral oil refinery and finished on a pleasant note with a social evening with the Ghanaian students and some German pupils. We left with many fond memories.

The final part of our trip ended with a short visit to Austria, where we pitched our tents alongside a lake close to Salzburg before starting the journey home with many stories to tell and new projects to complete. Personally, I realised that national education and school priorities were changing and that, at some point, I would be faced with difficult decisions.

I would like to think that I started my teaching career

with a clear pathway to reach the desired outcome. Looking back, I can almost justify every change as being part of a plan. My only problem is that, apart from wanting to be a teacher, I had no plan. My destiny was determined by chances that placed me in the right place at the right time. My limited experience of teaching the sixth form at Hinde House School had made me wish to do more sixth form teaching. This was at a time when Sheffield Council was planning to make all secondary schools comprehensive. One of the larger schools, Jordanthorpe, had a vacancy for an assistant head teacher. In anticipation of the possible development of sixth forms, the post advertisement identified post-16 experience would be an advantage. One of my colleagues showed me the advert and added the suggestion that I should apply. I didn't tell him that I was already composing my application! There were several months left before this post would commence so, considering the high level of doubt about my chances, I turned my mind back to really important things. After my appointment as Head of Upper School, a new teacher was appointed to my previous post of Head of Social Studies. His name was Gary Lycett and he had only just returned from Canada. I had known Gary before he left for Canada and I knew he would be a great asset to the school. He soon imbibed the culture of the school and together with Roger Smith and myself, enrolled as a supporter of Dave Cliffe's next project.

One morning, before the start of School, Dave asked the three of us if we would like to join him on a trip to Newark. We all agreed, and at the end of the day, we set off on the school bus on a 90-minute journey to our destination. As we drove, Dave explained the purpose of the trip. The school was close to the Sheffield canal and he had arranged the visit for us to see a barge that was for sale near Newark. When we arrived, we took a critical trip around Zelda, a large wooden barge, only to decide that it would be a costly project to repair. There was an air of disappointment on our return journey to Sheffield, but within a few days, Dave called us together to inform us that he had found a similar-sized steel barge available at Waddington's yard near Swinton. The story was that Mr. Waddington was approaching retirement and he appreciated our determination to involve our pupils in another challenging project that would lead to further opportunities for adventure. He explained that his barge, unusually, was made of stainless steel. It had served as a coal barge but was now surplus to requirement. With the folly of an eternal optimist and an everlasting spirit of adventure, with our blessing, Dave accepted the donation of the barge to the school. The barge was eventually delivered to the Sheffield Canal basin and the transformation into a classroom with accommodation for 24 was begun.

The first challenge was to cut port holes into the sides of the barge. Roger Smith was a brilliant metalwork teacher, but even his skill and available equipment were incapable of cutting stainless steel. Again, good fortune came to our rescue. The company, English Steel, was close to our school and many of the parents were employed there. As soon as they knew of our problem, they dispatched a team of welders with the appropriate equipment to cut the apertures needed to receive the port holes that had been built in the school metal workshop. Over the next few weeks, at the end of the school day, the school bus was regularly seen travelling along Attercliffe Common, carrying some teachers and pupils to the canal basin to continue the task of converting the barge. One day, the work group received a message that on the following day, they should bring some old clothes and, if possible, a shovel. Apparently, it was necessary to put a substantial amount of ballast into the front of the barge on which the washrooms could be constructed.

Soon after our arrival at the basin, a ready mix lorry fully loaded with concrete arrived. This was to be the last delivery of the day and the driver was disgruntled as he complained that he had been unable to have a break all day. After some discussion, it was agreed that he would put the shute from the lorry through the front port hole and that the 'labourers' would be on the inside of the barge with shovels ready to spread the concrete to maintain the balance. This seemed to be a sensible arrangement, but as the concrete started to flow, the driver went for a walk along the canal to enjoy a cigarette. Our knowledge of the rate of flow of concrete delivered by a ready mix lorry was almost non-existent but we soon found it could deliver faster than we could distribute it. Unfortunately, the 'labourers' inside the barge were unable to stop shovelling in order to find the driver to switch the delivery off! Very slowly, the barge tilted, and the water level of the canal came close to the open port holes. Fortunately, the driver returned to the lorry just in time to stop the delivery to avert a disaster. I suspect the driver left the basin with a few new words added to his vocabulary!

JORDANTHORPE
SCHOOL
SIXTH FORM PREFAB

The completion of the barge was significant because it coincided with my departure to take up my new post as deputy head teacher at Jordanthorpe School. I had spent seven very happy years working with brilliant colleagues serving youngsters from a deprived part of the city and from whom I had learned so much. Looking back, I realise that the period of my time at Park House witnessed the beginning of significant national changes. After the war, it was generally accepted that those pupils who attended a grammar school were destined to become leaders in public service, business or industry. They would follow the pipeline that started with initial qualifications at 16 that would allow access to further training and higher education with the added bonus of a steady increase in wealth throughout their lifetime. Of course, there were exceptions, and the 1944 Education

Act certainly allowed some bright youngsters from working-class backgrounds to take advantage of selective education. It was these fortunate young people who sowed the seeds of doubt about the fixed 'pool of ability' and the 'glass ceiling'. Most of my teacher colleagues, including myself, would identify themselves as being members of this group.

During the late 1960s, the developing global economy became increasingly competitive and knowledge-based. The focus of education policy began to change with an emphasis on the creation of a highly skilled workforce that would ensure that our economic performance was fit to compete with that of other advanced industrial nations. My arrival at Jordanthorpe was at a time of growing recognition that the UK's success and competitiveness was dependent on the application of knowledge and skills of a high order. James Callaghan, the Prime Minister, encapsulated the need for change in his speech at Ruskin College in 1976 when he expressed concerns that schools were failing to equip young people for work. He was responding to the concerns of many employers who criticised unaccountable teachers delivering an irrelevant curriculum. He stressed that education standards were not high enough and that schools were failing to prepare pupils for an increasingly complex world in which science, technology, numeracy and basic skills were generally given insufficient importance.

At Park House we had anticipated this change of emphasis when we created the examination group prior to the raising of the school leaving age to 16 in 1972. However, whilst pursuing this new priority, we maintained the importance of resilience and self-reliance, which would inspire our young people to dream the dream. I was determined to encourage these qualities in my new school.

As soon as I arrived at Jordanthorpe, it became clear that many parents had negative perceptions about the school, which were given much publicity in the local press. The decision of the Sheffield Council to make all secondary schools comprehensive was at the root of the problem. Jordanthorpe was a secondary modern school, but in the eyes of many parents, the former selective schools were deemed to be a more desirable destination for their children. The newspaper reports stressed that the parents felt that the lack of sixth form provision and the mistaken belief that the pupils were vandals and hooligans was a justification for their objections. The sixth form issue was a particular concern for the Councillors, many of whom had enjoyed the benefit of attending a selective school and they felt protective towards their old schools. Despite a commitment to equality, it was inconceivable that they would agree to close the sixth forms in the previously selective schools, so, in the interests of appearing to treat all schools equally, they decided that every school should be allowed to offer post-16 education. In reality they were concerned at the implications of this decision and, often with the support of education officers, set about dissuading many of the secondary modern schools from preparing proposals for such a development.

After my initial excitement at being appointed as a relatively young deputy Head Teacher with little experience in whole-school management, I began to realise the magnitude of my task. At first, I would sit in my office feeling inadequate but wanting to succeed. I could have taken the easy option and accepted that the school would be a mediocre comprehensive, but this would have contradicted the values that I was happy to embrace at the start of my career. It was at this point that I began to develop a strategy that was to be shaped over the next 25 years as Deputy Head and later as the Head Teacher. I have often been asked to explain this strategy and I always surprise people by explaining that I am a QPR supporter. I was born close to Loftus Road and all my family were supporters of the Club, not just when they were having success but also when the going was tough. I have witnessed the highs and, more usually, the lows, but I observed that in the good times, the team was always managed by a leader who could create a game plan, shared by every player, who understood their role and accountability for delivering success for the team. When this occurs, even 11 mediocre players can create success but when it is absent, 11 of the most skilled individuals will fail.

Unlike the manager of QPR, I identified just four key players or groups that needed to contribute to, share and implement a vision that would lead to success. They were the teachers, the pupils, the parents and the LEA. I soon identified that there were divisions amongst the staff. I had great respect for the Head Teacher, who had the unenviable task of managing the result of a previous decision made by the City Council. Until 1964 there were two Jordanthorpe Schools, one, for boys and the other for girls. Each school had its own Head Teacher. In 1964, the Council made the decision to amalgamate the two schools under one Head Teacher. There was clear rivalry between the teachers from each school, who were obviously concerned about which of the existing Head Teachers would be appointed to take charge of the new school. The eventual successful candidate was Miss Irene Prebble, previously of the Girls' School, who had the unenviable task of managing a clearly divided and resentful group of teachers. When I arrived at the school the problem was still a live issue and one that urgently needed addressing. In a short period of time, I established a good working relationship with the Head, which allowed me to take the lead in creating a strategy to address the issues the school faced. The unity of the staff was my first priority and it was clear that my own credibility was critical if I was to ask for commitment,

Ken Cook, Gordon Gosling, Chris Parratt,
Mick Gizzy, on the road, ready for adventure

Early morning departure from Boulogne Youth Hostel

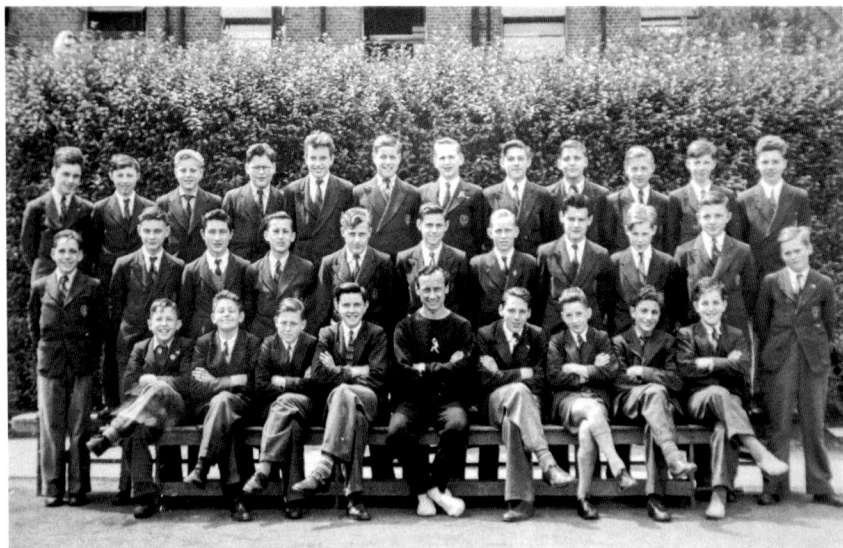

Early days at St. Clement Danes with form teacher Bernard McCarthy

Resting after a long journey with Bernard McCarthy (Teacher)

Serious sixth form students, with Jack Harvey (Teacher)

Coleridge Road School – my class 1962-3

My colleagues at Park House, Mr. Aizlewood (Headteacher)
middle of front row. On his right, John Philips (Deputy Head)

21/02 Nr. 173 / Freitag, 30. Juli 1971 **WAZ**

OBERBÜRGERMEISTER CLAUS empfing am Donnerstag die Besuchergruppe aus der Partnerstadt Sheffield. Die jungen Besucher diskutierten mit dem Stadtoberhaupt über Arbeit und Aufgaben einer deutschen Großstadt. Am gleichen Tage konnte die Gruppe bei der Besichtigung der Ausstellung „650 Jahre Stadt Bochum" einen Blick in die Stadtgeschichte werfen.

A greeting from the Oberbürgermeister on arrival in Bochum

Meeting new friends – our reception in Bochum

Unstone Grange nature lesson – Dave Cliffe

Unstone Grange – back to the real world but with fond memories

Dave Cliffe and Roger Smith with a group of pupils
planning the conversion of the barge

Vandalism allegations denied

By a staff reporter

GOVERNORS of Jordanthorpe Comprehensive School, Sheffield, are worried about a fall in the number of children going there from Sir Harold Jackson Junior School—one of the school's feeders.

Three-quarters of the parents of children in their final year at Sir Harold Jackson have opted for schools other than Jordanthorpe, which is far higher than at any of Jordanthorpe's other feeders.

Vice-chairman of the Jordanthorpe governors, Mr. Robert Jackson, said today he had been to see several parents and found that lack of a sixth-form at the school was the reason.

"I have two girls attending the school and I take great exception to allegations of vandalism at the school being one of the reasons," he said.

"I consider the school, under the headship of Miss I. E. V. Prebble, to be one of the best behaved schools in the area and that my daughters are receiving a very good education," he added.

Sheffield education committee are currently examining a twinning of sixth-forms throughout the city and Jordanthorpe would then share a sixth-form with Rowlinson.

Sixth-form D-I-Y waits for go-ahead

A do-it-yourself sixth form centre at Jordanthorpe Comprehensive, Sheffield, could be in use by the end of the year if the scheme is given the go-ahead by the authorities.

The school has found a pre-fabricated building at Dore which it hopes to dismantle and re-erect at the school but first it needs planning permission and the approval of the Education Committee.

The cost to the school will be between £400 and £500. They decided to provide their own sixth form centre because there are no funds available from the education authority

Morning Telegraph 17th September 1973.

CHAPTER 6

Not all parents objected

CHAPTER 6

Waiting for a decision

Sheffield parents give school cold shoulder

By a staff reporter

PARENTS of children at a Sheffield junior school are cold-shouldering the comprehensive school which their children are expected to attend. One of the reasons is said to be concern over the incidence of hooliganism.

FROM LAST MONDAY'S STAR.

Hooliganism charge 'unjustified'

THE FOLLOWING LETTER, FROM JOAN M. WARD AND W. WALTON, HAS BEEN WRITTEN ON BEHALF OF 48 OTHER MEMBERS OF THE STAFF OF JORDANTHORPE SCHOOL, INCLUDING THE HEADMISTRESS (MISS I. PREBBLE), WHO HAVE ALSO SIGNED IT:

THE STAFF of Jordanthorpe School protest most strongly against the remark of Councillor Frank Adams, reported in The Star on Monday. He makes the totally unjustified charge of hooliganism in this school and suggests that it is a factor guiding parents in their desire to send their children to other schools.

It is apparent that a small but vociferous group, in order to achieve its aims, has instituted a smear campaign into which it is attempting to draw any councillor who is willing to make ill-informed and thoughtless statements.

Councillor Adams is a member of the Education Committee, and from his statements the public might be led to believe that he is speaking from personal or inside information. As the people most closely involved with the pupils of this school, we wish to state that his allegation is not only unfounded, but is a slur on past and present pupils, parents and staff, who value the good name of Jordanthorpe.

We welcome the fact that the Chairman of the Education Committee has rejected Councillor Adams' allegation, but are concerned that The Star should publish such statements without approaching the school.

We should be obliged, therefore, if you would publish our letter in full, and we invite your reporter to visit us so that he can present a truthful report of the activities and conduct of our pupils.

CHAPTER 6

Parental antagonism and justifications

JORDANTHORPE Comprehensive, in Sheffield is on the lookout for second-hand huts.

The school has written to local builders asking if they have any redundant huts which they can offer to the school at a reasonable price.

The school needs a decent - sized hut to create a sixth - form centre. It is one of two Sheffield comprehensives which have been given the go-ahead to develop a sixth form from scratch. And although it has classroom space to cope with the extra pupils, it needs extra accommodation for private study and tutorial rooms.

The head, Miss Ivy Prebble, said: "We do want somewhere which is specifically for the sixth form and we are trying every avenue we can think of."

She added that she was

Sixth form in search of a hut

confident that the appeal would produce results.

"We have decided to help ourselves to provide at least a temporary centre," she added.

In the letter to builders, the school points out that while other comprehensives with sixth forms have been able to develop purpose built centres, Jordanthorpe is launching its new sixth form at a time when the local education authority has been forced to make cuts in its budget.

"You can never tell how temporary things will be these days, but we are not complaining. I am sure that once we have got a hut we can make a first - class centre out of it," said Miss Prebble.

CHAPTER 6

They said no, we said yes!

Ken Cook with Helen Sharman at Sheffield University

Staff group at Meadowhead just before my retirement

Sixth form for school would cost £40,000

Morning Telegraph
Education Correspondent

It would cost over £40,000 to set up a sixth form at Jordanthorpe comprehensive in Sheffield and £25,000 a year to run it.

The figures are quoted in a special report on the feasibility of launching a new sixth form at the school — an idea which could set the pattern for the development of sixth form and post-16 education in the city.

The estimated cost for a sixth form at Jordanthorpe is likely to be cheaper than the cost of setting up sixth forms at other comprehensives as the school already has spare accommodation.

The running costs are made up largely of the salaries of the extra teachers who would be needed to staff a sixth form.

Teachers

The cost of the operation may lead to second thoughts within Sheffield's Education Committee, particularly as other schools in the city are asking to join Jordanthorpe in founding a sixth form rather than contributing to the existing group sixth form system.

Another factor which has yet to be taken into account is the possible effect of a sixth form at Jordanthorpe on the sixth form at Rowlinson which it now feeds.

The report will now go to the working party of teachers and education officials for their comments.

Last night, Coun Frank Adams, Conservative spokesman on education, attacked the idea: "The committee is trying to expand at a time when we have not got the money to do properly what we are already committed to."

PUPIL GOVERNORS GIVEN CONFIDENTIAL SCHOOL PAPERS

By **JOHN IZBICKI**, *Education Correspondent*

TEACHERS at a large comprehensive school were up in arms when two of their pupils were given official permission to examine confidential application forms for their school's headship.

Both pupils—a girl aged 15 and a boy of 17—are on the board of governors of Sheffield's Jordanthorpe Comprehensive whose headmistress, Miss I. E. V. Prebble, is to retire.

Applications for her job are due to be shortlisted next week and each governor has received a letter from Mr George Harrison, Sheffield's chief education officer, informing them that application forms could be inspected prior to that meeting.

The two pupil governors also received the letter and immediately demanded to see the confidential files. With such official backing their request was hard to refuse.

But as soon as the teachers of the 1,160-pupil school heard of the decision, they called an emergency meeting and voted unanimously against it. They strongly disapproved of pupils being allowed to help pick a teacher or head.

Available for perusal

Mr L. S. Brown, senior assistant education officer, confirmed yesterday that every Sheffield secondary school had two pupil governors on their boards as well as representatives of parents, teaching and non-teaching staffs.

"Under our new Articles of Government of schools, the whole governing body is involved in shortlisting staff. There is nothing to prevent pupils who are governors from taking part.

"If a board of governors decided to concentrate only certain representative sections on shortlisting a job, then that is their business. Clearly, sensitivities differ from one school to another."

Mr Brown said that all governors at Jordanthorpe were invited to attend the shortlisting. "We informed them that copies of the application forms were available at the school for perusal before the meeting," he added.

He said that following the staff protest both staff and pupil governors have decided not to take part in the shortlisting.

Mr Peter Smith, assistant secretary of the 42,000-strong Assistant Masters' Association said last night "I have never heard of anything like this. Industrial democracy has its virtues but whether it should apply to pupils in schools is a matter of doubt."

CHAPTER 6
Justification not to implement a clear political decision

CHAPTER 6
Problems about involvement of elected pupil governor in the appointment of the new Headteacher

School gets the cold shoulder

Morning Telegraph Reporter

A Sheffield comprehensive has been cold-shouldered by the parents of children at one of its feeder primary schools.

Threequarters of the children from Sir Harold Jackson school, Bradway—who should go to Jordanthorpe — are being sent to other comprehensives by their parents.

The parents have made use of the city's parental choice scheme to send their children to King Ecgbert—or to Rowlinson.

Lack of a sixth form at Jordanthorpe—and the fact that it takes many children from local council housing estates—are thought to be behind the rejection by the Bradway parents.

No problems

Coun Peter Horton, chairman of the Education Committee, said the opting-out would not cause Jordanthorpe any problems as it was rather full.

A scheme was being considered for splitting the feed from Sir Harold Jackson between King Ecgbert and Jordanthorpe as "Jordanthorpe is rather full while King Ecgbert's has vacancies," he added.

IE 12 **By a staff reporter**

PARENTS of children at a Sheffield junior school are cold-shouldering the comprehensive school which their children are expected to attend. One of the reasons is said to be concern over the incidence of hooliganism.

Only a quarter of the children in their final year at Sir Harold Jackson Junior School, Bradway (17 out of 68) are to attend Jordanthorpe Comprehensive, for which the school is supposed to be a feeder.

Most of the other parents have opted for King Ecgbert or Rowlinson Comprehensives, only a short distance from Jordanthorpe.

Conservative Coun. Frank Adams, a member of Sheffield education committee, said it was originally planned that the school should feed King Ecgbert's.

"I have had some discussions with the education chairman and education officials, and I understand they are trying to split that area so that some of the children will automatically go to King Ecgbert's," he said.

"It is not purely the question of lack of a sixth form at Jordanthorpe, but there is the question of geographical location, and the incidence of hooliganism is a contributory factor."

Education chairman Coun. Peter Horton admitted that the possibility of splitting the feed from Sir Harold Jackson between Jordanthorpe and King Ecgbert's was being considered as "Jordanthorpe is rather full while King Ecgbert's has vacancies."

He rejected the claim that there was any more hooliganism at Jordanthorpe than at any other large comprehensive school in the city.

They always blame us . . .

I WISH to protest at the unjust way in which pupils at Jordanthorpe school are treated.

I say, unjust, because when people talk of the unruly hooligans at

The Star 2nd December 1974.

Meadowhead who push at bus stops, swear and shout, it is always the Jordanthorpe pupils who are condemned, and never those from Rowlinson, the neighbouring school.

Naturally, any school has a percentage of pupils who refuse to be ordered into good behaviour, just in defiance against the rules, but as a Jordanthorpe pupil, I think that my school is lucky to have only a few of these people.

In my opinion, Jordanthorpe has a good standard of pupils to match a high standard of teaching.

We are criticised for the bad things we supposedly do, but there is never a mention of us entertaining spina bifida children, helping the aged, and Christmas shopping expeditions for the elderly.

Pupil

The transfer of responsibility, Irene Prebble (retiring Headteacher),
to Ken Cook (newly appointed Headteacher)

Staff group at Jordanthorpe just after
my appointment as Headteacher

Ken Cook with former pupils Helen Sharman and Sarah Burdekin
who later become Head of the sixth form at Meadowhead

Team spirit amongst the teaches, lots of optimism, not matched by results!

Anybody got a hut going spare?

DO you know of any spare prefabricated hut or building?

If you do, a bunch of do-it-yourself sixth-formers at Jordanthorpe School, Sheffield, would like to get in touch.

At present they have only an overcrowded 40-year-old wooden hut from Tennessee in which to relax at break and lunch-times.

But the nine-strong sixth form committee aim to change that. They have already raised £1,000 towards a new social centre and are now looking round for a building.

"Someone, somewhere, must have a redundant building or will let us have one cheap," said committee member Chris McQueen.

Since the sixth form opened in 1973, pupil numbers have risen from 20 ·

120, and are expected to rise again next year.

"We're so crowded in the old hut," said Chris, aged 17, of Birchitt Road, Bradway. "There is no way you can have a social centre when you are on top of one another."

Sixth-formers have to spend their free time in the ramshackle hut, a converted room behind the school stage, or the library.

Attitude

Said committeee member Jim Wilkinson, aged 18, of Kenwell Drive, Bradway: "We look at other sixth forms and get envious at times. What we want we have to work hard for."

The money they have raised has come from discos, sponsored sports events and 'uck shop which they run.

They are quick to point out they have also helped with remedial teaching at the school and organised discos for younger pupils.

Headmaster Ken Cook said: "These sixth-formers are prepared to do something for themselves. It is an important part of the attitude of the school.

"The complaint is not against the education authority. We accept that the money isn't available and we don't expect them to do anything for us.

"The problem is one which affects the whole school — and that is overcrowding."

In the picture are committee members (from left) Rosalind Hall, Chris McQueen, Tim Freeman, Elizabeth Waters, Alan Vragg, Jim Wilkinson, hn Patrick and Neil Tilley.

New sixth formers but with the old spirit, we will find a way!

Move justified, says city head

By Clark Herron,
Education reporter

FROM secondary modern to Oxford and Cambridge — that is the path trodden by Sheffield's Jordanthorpe Comprehensive.

Two pupils have just won entry to the prestigious "Oxbridge stakes," the first of Jordanthorpe's all-comprehensive sixth-form to do so. They are: Adam Bennett, headed for Cambridge, and Andrew Woods, Oxford.

Eighteen others in the 32-strong sixth-form are going on to degree courses at other universities or at polytechnics. The remaining 12 all have jobs.

Jordanthorpe was one of the first to set up a sixth-form in a move five years ago to have them at all city comprehensives.

Headmaster Mr. Ken Cook claims the figures show the idea — and comprehensive education — is working: "Of the first group to go through the sixth, 17 gained degrees this year. Coupled with the university or polytechnic entrance record for this year, the figures justify the decision taken five years ago.

"There are more important things than just getting one or two pupils into Oxbridge," he went on. "But we can now start developing links with them. Pupils from schools with a history of getting people into Oxbridge stand a better chance. If selection were just on ability, we could have people in easily."

CHAPTER 7
We were right!

CHAPTER 8
Visitors from Japan visiting our school to discover
the factors that helped us succeed

CHAPTER 8
A farewell from the leader of the Japanese visitors,
departing for their tour of schools in Europe

SHEFFIELD
TELEGRAPH

Number 407, Friday, July 18, 1997

Forty five pence

CHAPTER 8

Celebration of the Ofsted 'outstanding' judgement. David Blunkett plays with the school orchestra

BLOWING HIS OWN TRUMPET: Education Secretary and Brightside MP David Blunkett took the opportunity to get in tune with Meadowhead School band on Monday. The secondary has been highlighted by inspectors as one of the top 16 schools in Yorkshire and Humberside.

SANCTUARY BUILDINGS GREAT SMITH STREET
WESTMINSTER LONDON SW1P 3BT
TELEPHONE 0171 925 5000

The Rt Hon GILLIAN SHEPHARD MP

The Headteacher
Meadowhead School
Dyche Lane
SHEFFIELD
S8 8BR

Dear Headteacher,

10 FEB 1997

Your OFSTED inspection report shows yours to be an outstandingly
successful school. Your achievement has rightly been recognised
in the Annual Report of Her Majesty's Chief Inspector of
Schools. I am writing to congratulate you, your governing body,
staff, parents and pupils for this achievement.

I know how much hard work has gone into producing this very high
standard of performance. I very much hope we will be able to
draw on your experience to help other schools.

Yours ever,

Gillian Shephard

GILLIAN SHEPHARD

D/EE

CHAPTER 8

Recognition from the Secretary of State for Education

Ken Cook is retiring after 21 years as head of Jordanthorpe and Meadowhead Schools. He talked to **Lesley Draper**

Ken Cook at Meadowhead who is Sheffield's longest serving headteacher and an inspiration to thousands of children

From the school of hard knocks

WHEN young Ken Cook was threatened with expulsion from secondary school it never occurred to him that one day he would be Sheffield's longest-serving headteacher, in charge of the city's largest comprehensive and an inspiration to thousands of young people.

The pasting he got from his father was a lesson Ken has never forgotten. In fact he admits: "My dad was the biggest influence in my life. He had to leave school at 13 and was unemployed during the Depression. He used to cycle miles, five nights a week, to get the qualifications to become a teacher. He made that commitment because he placed immense value on education, and that's what he did for me."

Ken followed in his father's footsteps and went off to train as a teacher in Leicester, where he met his wife, Jennifer, now a teacher at Ridgeway.

"I wanted to go back to London once we'd qualified and she wanted to come to Sheffield, so we compromised and came to Sheffield," he grins.

"That was the best thing I ever did. The difference between London and Sheffield is the people and that's one of the things I've appreciated since I came here. I'd never go back now."

His first post was at Coleridge Road Secondary Modern Boys' School in Attercliffe, teaching English, history and PE as well as his specialist subjects, maths and geography.

"It was an education to me – I couldn't understand a word the kids said! But they were real people. They'd seen tough times, but there was work, so education wasn't so important to them."

He moved to Norfolk School and to Park House; at 26, head of Social Studies. "I remember the Raising Of the School Leaving Age. The year before, I knocked on the door of every child and asked their parents if they realised their youngster was capable of getting CSEs or O-levels.

"We got 20 to stay on voluntarily and they were our first group to take external exams – they did well, too. The parents had never even considered they might stay on. It was a matter of turning the system."

In 1973 Ken was appointed deputy head of Jordanthorpe secondary modern. He had believed he was being interviewed for the post of third assistant head. "If I'd realised it was for deputy head I don't think I'd even have dared apply for it!"

His first task was to set up a sixth form – and to provide a centre where the youngsters would be based. The LEA refused to fund the project, but Ken managed to obtain an old wartime prefab and spent every evening, weekend and holiday working on it.

"There were 15 youngsters in our first sixth form," he recalls. "They came along and helped dig. The foundations were four feet deep and the building was 40-foot square, so it was a big job."

The nearby dual carriageway was under construction at the time and the Irish foreman took pity on the young workers. He sent in council diggers to excavate the foundations, then a convoy of lorries to shift the debris – now buried beneath the central reservation of the Bochum Parkway. His men also mucked in to lay the concrete base.

Men from the Works Department, who were carrying out maintenance work at the school, also took pity on the youngsters. They returned in the evening and laid 8,000 bricks.

"It cost me 200 cigarettes and a bottle of whisky," says Ken. "It always makes

> 'It was an education I couldn't understand a word the kids said! But they were real people. They'd seen tough times' – Ken Cook

me chuckle because the authority said there was no money for this, then they did the work anyway!"

The building served the sixth form for many years, although it eventually had to be demolished because of its asbestos cladding. Ken, though, is made of more enduring stuff and has remained at the school – now amalgamated with neighbouring Rowlinson – ever since.

"The amalgamation was the biggest challenge I had ever faced," he admits. "We had three sites, 136 teachers and two sets of support staff, as well as over 3,000 pupils. To come through that and the school be as successful as it has been is quite an achievement."

T o d a y Meadowhead has 85 teachers and a streamlined 1600 students. Exam results are going from strength to strength – in the past five years the proportion of high grade GCSEs has almost doubled – and last year the school won special commendation from HM Inspector following its Ofsted report.

"The biggest challenge since amalgamation has been to ensure quality," says Ken. It's a challenge he takes very seriously and the way forward, he believes, is through 'community support and involvement'. "A community feeling good about itself raises aspirations, so my view is that you've got to go out there and do something about that community."

Meadowhead has already started down this path with the launch of a summer literacy school.

Ken has put his now-famous fundraising tactics to good effect and has gathered sufficient money to run a two-week course for nine and ten-year-olds this summer. He hopes to attract lottery money to establish a regular programme over the next three years.

The initiative will also involve parents and helpers, working on an accredited basis to draw the community closer together and bring adults back into the system.

"It's uniting people who need skills and people who have skills – whether it's fishing, or crafts, or reading.

"It's wonderful in my view. It's saying that people who haven't been working have a value and we can recognise it."

So enthusiastic is Ken that he has every intention of remaining involved with the scheme, despite his imminent retirement.

"I won't cause the new head any problems, but I feel committed to the scheme and I want to see it through.

"I really believe the future for successful schools lies in working very closely with their communities, so I've got a point to prove."

At 57 – and after 21 years as head of the same school – he believes the time has now come for a change.

"There's no doubt his dad would be proud of him."

At the Cutlers Hall, Sheffield, receiving recognition from
Richard Field OBE, Master Cutler of my ten years of service
as Chairman of the Education Business Partnership and
membership in the Strategic Education Forum

Telephone: (0114) 272 6444
Fax: (0114) 273 6279

Sheffield
City Council

Jonathan Crossley-Holland

Our reference:
Our reference: JCH

All enquiries to:
Telephone: 0114 273 5726

Date: 16 July 1999

Education

Executive Director Education
Jonathan Crossley-Holland

Education Department
Leopold Street
Sheffield
S1 1RJ

Mr. K. Cook
Headteacher
Fir Vale School

012107

Dear Ken

There will be other opportunities too, but I just wanted to record formally on behalf of the LEA my gratitude for what you have achieved at Fir Vale over the last year. This has come on top of many other contributions to the City's education service, defined in the broadest sense.

In many ways, Earl Marshal had become a symbol of all the dysfunctionalism in the Council, the Education Service and Secondary education.

It has now become the opposite – a symbol of what can be achieved. This is principally down to you with your unique style of very personal leadership. You also dug me, and the LEA, out of a hole!

I am delighted about your appointment to the Leadership Centre and I look forward to continuing collaboration.

Yours sincerely

Jonathan Crossley-Holland
Executive Director Education

Copy: Cllr. Sylvia Anginotti
    Cllr. Colin Ross
    Keith Pollard, Chair of Governors, Fir Vale School
    Directorate
    Yvonne Roberts

CHAPTER 10

Saturday interview

with Carolyn Waudby

CHURCHILL and Sir John Harvey-Jones are Ken Cook's mentors.

Energetic, passionate, committed, decisive, as head of Meadowhead School for 21 years and the man who was hauled in from semi-retirement to pull the former Earl Marshal School up by the bootstraps, it is easy to see why.

"I've always admired Churchill because he led through very difficult times. He made sense of what didn't make sense. That means being quite ruthless at times.

"He looked at the outcome and thought about how to achieve it. He is a good example of someone who cut through the dross."

It is the team philosophy espoused by Sir John Harvey-Jones he identifies with - the idea that everyone has a role to play in the successful working of an organisation.

"If I were a football manager I could have the 11 best, star players in the world and we still wouldn't win. I'm a QPR fan so that comes from the heart.

"It's very important each player knows what they've got to do or they're letting the rest of the team down. A group of very ordinary players can be made very successful."

KEN Cook is Sheffield's answer to the Lenny Henry character in the television series Hope and Glory. He was pulled out of semi-retirement to captain the 'fresh start' Fir Vale School. But his early life in education was less promising - he was almost thrown out of Grammar School as a lad.

We're not going to be anything less than the best

❝I wanted teachers that were confident in their subject❞

Meadowhead School was one of only 20 secondary schools in the country to gain the OFSTED accolade of being an "outstanding school" just before Ken retired.'

But he says himself it will be his year as head of Fir Vale School (formerly Earl Marshal School) which he will be remembered for.

Earl Marshal School in Grimesthorpe was closed down and branded a failure in a blaze of negative publicity. It was relaunched a year ago under the new name Fir Vale with Ken as the headteacher. Six other candidates were turned down because they were considered not up to the job.

Rumour has it that because Ken's retirement package would have been affected by the salary for the headteacher's job, he did it for nothing - but this has never been confirmed.

A year on a new, permanent head has been appointed and Ken, 59, is moving on to become the director of the South Yorkshire Leadership School based at Hallam University - a centre for training headteachers and school middle managers which is hoping to become the national nerve-knot for new Government initiative.

He admits he will be sad to leave Fir Vale. "I've enjoyed seeing the pupils grow in maturity because they've been made to be accountable. I think the school is on track now. The potential is very high indeed."

The job was challenging to say the least. Children were fighting in dinner queues, teachers were out of the classroom.

Ninety per cent of the pupils at Fir Vale are Muslim but Ken stresses the "things that are important" are the same, no matter what the community is.

"We have an interesting mix, children just arrived here without English. We have got to provide for them. We're talking about youngsters, quite bright but because of their English skills they've had a problem. We've got to work on their language ability but you don't do that in isolation."

Before addressing the school's problems he talked to the parents and people in the community. The message was unanimous. They wanted a well disciplined school with an emphasis on achievement.

In true Churchillian style he says his message to the school was: "We're not going to be anything less than the best. It's not optional."

Accountability is Ken's buzz word. "You don't go looking for innovative curricular developments. I wanted teachers that were confident in their subject."

He put "accountable systems" in place including discipline codes posted up on walls - with the consequences for pupils if they went against them. He explains it's all about "choices and consequences" - a popular theme for his assemblies.

"What happens today is that excuses are made for young people. They are old enough to make decisions. I think we shield them from consequences. The consequence may not be a punishment. It may be something positive.

"What I found was the pupils were very loyal to the school. The community desperately wanted the school to succeed. What was missing was the very clear leadership."

He tells with pride stories of taking visitors around the school who comment on how disciplined the pupils are - and occasions when the school was "crawling" with OFSTED inspectors, to whom the children kept saying, do you like our school?"

Ken only reads to rationalise his way of thinking - books such as The Fifth Dimension by Peter Senge and Stephen Covey's The Seven Habits of Highly Effective People - apart from the odd biography at Christmas.

He speaks about the "law of exact opposites" - ideas that were meant to help people from non-privileged backgrounds but which did the reverse, such as Comprehensive Education, Open University, the GCSE exam and school League Tables.

The latter makes him particularly angry. "We've taken youngsters from war torn areas of the world such as Somalia, Ethiopia and the Yemen and turned out good citizens. These youngsters still want to engage in a system that's rejected them at every stage."

He himself came from a large family which lived in a council house in Shepherd's Bush, London. He was about to be thrown out of Grammar School for not working when a teacher introduced him to cycling. With teams of classmates he went youth hostelling around the country every year.

"I met new people and new places. That teacher showed me another way and that saved me."

A philanthropist through and through, he talks of one occasion that stands out above all others. It was when he presented Basic Skills certificates to adults at Fir Vale School. Sheffield College had arranged for a teaching unit to be based at the school since many adults in the area could not speak English at all. He was deeply moved.

"Everything I ever stood for happened on that day."

CHAPTER 10

TELEGRAPH NEWS

Sheffield Telegraph, Friday, July 16, 19[...]

New challenge as Ken pushes back boundaries

By LESLEY DRAPER

HEADTEACHER Ken Cook (pictured) who came out of semi-retirement to launch Fir Vale School, steps down from the post this month.

But he is taking on an equally challenging role – as director of the new South Yorkshire Leadership Centre, based at Hallam University. The centre, to be officially launched in September, will offer training and guidance for headteachers and senior managers throughout the county.

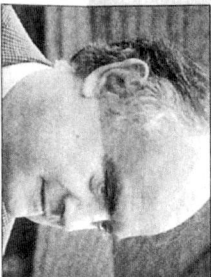

"It's a job that will really push the boundaries back," said Mr Cook. "My job is to set it up, get it on a proper financial footing and get things moving."

The idea was put forward by headteachers in Sheffield's Education Action Zone, who approached Hallam University to help them improve leadership skills.

The university's Head of Education, Di Bentley, suggested establishing a county-wide initiative and a steering group was established involving secondary heads and education advisors from across South Yorkshire.

The proposals have been welcomed by schools, which have come under increasing pressure to raise standards in recent years. Already almost 90% of Sheffield schools have signed up to use the centre and its services – and Mr Cook is confident that number will increase.

"I hope we're going to get to the point where every school will see this as a natural thing to be part of."

But he warned there were no quick fixes: "What you won't get is the gimmicky Anthony Robbins types. It's solid work that makes schools successful."

The centre will be modelled on one run by the Institute of Education in London.

"I've a view as to how it should develop, which doesn't necessarily coincide wit[h] what's gone before," said Mr Cook.

On a trip to Budapest in Hungary, h[e] was impressed with the way the[y] approach brought together groups from across the education spectrum, includin[g] headteachers, LEA advisors and acad[e]mics.

"I'm interested in going in that dire[c]tion," he admitted. "Some people ar[e] born with leadership skills, but there [is] more than that to being a good leade[r]. Part of it is recognising people who ar[e] good at what they do and getting them [...] share that with others."

Teachers get hi-tech lesson in leadership

SOUTH Yorkshire's leading teachers are set to receive the very latest professional training, thanks to a new initiative launched today.

The north's first regional Centre for School Leadership, based at Sheffield Hallam University, was opened by Education Secretary David Blunkett.

The aim is to give heads and senior teachers the most up-to-date training opportunities to develop skills that will make them more effective in their jobs.

Mr Blunkett sees such centres as another key factor in the drive to push up school standards.

Electronic

Director of the South Yorkshire Leadership Centre is Ken Cook, former head at Sheffield's Meadowhead and Fir Vale schools.

He said the centre was a new idea as it would create a learning network, rather than exist as a physical set of offices.

"Its base is at Sheffield Hallam, but most of the learning will take place in the workplace or on line," he said.

"To make this point we created an electronic 'virtual plaque' for the Secretary of State to unveil to activate our new website."

Mr Blunkett said centres

Leading by example: Director Ken Cook, vice-chancellor Prof Di Green and David Blunkett MP

By Mike Russell

white charger – it's about teamwork in schools. We need to build management and leadership skills and schools must share those resources."

Partnership

"No one individual can make a school successful – a

their careers. Their opinions on key issues will be sought.

Mr Cook said the centre would aim to benefit the region's economy too.

It will work closely with all four county education authorities and with Hallam's business and education schools.

The Sheffield centre will be

CHAPTER 11

High-tech tool to raise standards

WITH the click of a button Education Secretary David Blunkett unveiled a "virtual" plaque, appropriately marking the launch of Sheffield's new high-tech training centre for senior teachers.

The South Yorkshire Leadership Centre, based at Hallam University's Collegiate Crescent campus, will put the county at the cutting edge of educational development.

It aims to tap into excellence, drawing on the expertise of some of the nation's top names and promoting collaboration between different sections of the educational community.

Although based in university offices, the centre will exist primarily as a team-ing network, supporting its users through courses in the workplace or on line via computer links.

Mr Blunkett sees it as a further tool in his drive to raise standards. "Leadership is about motivating and stimulating the talent and the commitment and the con-tribution of everyone in the service," he told an audience of educationalists.

Ken Cook, Vice Chancellor Diana Green and David Blunkett

"This centre is about sharing through virtual technology the expertise and excellence that exists. It's about being able to identify best practice and ensure people can draw down on it very quickly."

The work of the new centre will be

fundamental in developing skills and building on successful initiatives at the heart of Government education policy, he said.

"We have the potential to be able to transform Britain's education service into the best in the world. With this kind of

project we're making a start and laying the foundations."

The South Yorkshire Leadership Centre is underwritten by Hallam University, but it hopes to be self-financ-ing within a year, securing funding from the Government, Europe and by running courses and conferences.

Its director is Ken Cook, for 21 years head of Meadowhead School and latterly head of Sheffield's first "fresh start" comprehensive, Fir Vale.

Ultimately he aims to establish a team of top headteachers, LEA advisors and university personnel, working on an interchangeable basis.

The official launch presented an opportunity to demonstrate the technol-ogy which will play a central role in the centre's operation. Teachers from Slough took part in the event via a video link. There was also a successful link-up with former Sheffield-based professor Andy Hargreaves, speaking from Toronto, Canada.

ISSUE NO. 2 AUGUST 2002

crusader

the newsletter of **St John Ambulance** in Derbyshire

New Commander

Derbyshire St John Ambulance has a new Commander, Ken Cook CBE, and this Cook hopes he has the recipe for our success.

Coming from a background of improving failing schools, the new commander hopes he can use his experiences to ensure Derbyshire St John is a first class organisation.

Mr Cook, who lives in Dronfield and is currently a self-employed education consultant, has been a teacher and headteacher in secondary schools in the Sheffield area for 41 years.

He headed the Meadowhead School (an amalgamation of Jordanthorpe and Rowlinson schools) for 21 years, transforming it into an OFSTED-acclaimed "outstanding school".
More recently he also took over and turned around the named-and-shamed Earl Marshal School, reinstating it as one of the most successful examples of a "fresh start" school in the country.

On retiring from the active school environment, he founded the Centre for Leadership in Education in partnership with the four South Yorkshire LEAs and Sheffield Hallam University. He was director there for three years.
At the same time he was acting as a consultant working with LEAs and schools across the country.

He has held a number of appointments as a school governor, governor of Sheffield Hallam University, chairman of the Sheffield Education and Business Partnership, and is a member of the South Yorkshire Learning and Skills Council.
He was appointed a Commander of the British Empire (CBE) in 2000 for services to education.

Most importantly, he comes from a family with strong connections to St John Ambulance. His father was involved in SJA for many years and ran first aid training at his workplace throughout his career.

It is this link that led to Ken's interest in leading Derbyshire St John: "It is a bit to do with pay-back. I have had an interesting career and I think ensuring the continued success of St John is similar to my work in schools. I hope I can now give something back to the organisation.

"This is a big commitment and it is a bit daunting but also a challenge; but I have taken on big commitments before and succeeded.
"Volunteering is very different to what is was 20 or 30 years ago. I want to respect the organisation's traditions while also moving to the future and making sure Derbyshire St John is delivering a first class service and the best it can possibly achieve.

"There are some superb people in the organisation and it will be a pleasure to work with them – it often astounds me that so many people so selflessly give their time and commitment to something that is a massive community resource. There is very strong potential for Derbyshire St John Ambulance. I want it to become one of the best SJA counties in the country," he said.

Mr Cook is setting himself until November to learn about St John Ambulance and the Derbyshire members. He also hopes to have visited all the units by the end of the year. He will hold the temporary title as Commander (designate) until his appointment is officially confirmed by the Priory in October. The Chief Commander, Peter Brown has already approved his appointment.

When it comes to plans for Derbyshire St John, Mr Cook will be looking at the structure to see whether changes need to be made:
"Winston Churchill once said 'We shape our buildings and thereafter our buildings shape us'. When you've got a structure that should be providing and delivering a service, you have to look at it to see if it is working effectively. At the end of the day we have to be offering a service that has a first class quality about it; we owe that to the volunteers and the public we support. The volunteers are absolutely crucial in that, and I will ensure those volunteers are supported, while at the same time supporting the commercial and fundraising side which in turn helps to support the volunteers."

But the greatest passion for the 62-year-old married father-of-two is his beloved football club the Queens Park Rangers – a link he retains from his childhood in London.... Still, we shouldn't hold that against him!

Inside

Caring for Life

CHAPTER 12

Moving On...

Monday 20th December 2010

After three years in post, one of the St John's Ambulance most respected members has retired from his role as Chair of Council.

Ken Cook, from Dronfield and a former Sheffield Headteacher, has been a leading influence within St John Ambulance Derbyshire since 2002 when he joined as Commander.

Ken Cook receives his plaque from Chair of Council (Designate) Dr Cheryle Berry.

He took on the Top Job of leading the County's 1300 uniformed volunteers in 2007 and is now moving to other projects.

Renowned for his hands-on approach and respected for his leadership skills, one of Ken's greatest legacies was restructuring the governing Council, which he reformed by bringing in experts and making it more proactive.

Under his leadership, Derbyshire became established as an influence within the organisation nationally and made an impact on a broader scale too, setting up a foundation degree in volunteer management in partnership with the **University of Derby**. Through this, a number of SJA staff and volunteers went on to gain BA and MA degrees.

Ken now plans to return to studying himself, working towards a doctorate in leadership and management at the University of Derby, where he is a governor. He also plans to develop other interests including a role with **Derby NHS Trust**.

He will be succeeded as **Chair of Council by Dr Cheryle Berry**, who paid tribute to Ken's commitment and leadership at a reception last week.

She said: "We have been extremely fortunate to have Ken as Commander and more recently Chair of Council. He has brought many new initiatives into the organisation as well as upholding its traditions.

"His style and leadership have set a very high benchmark, making Derbyshire one of the leading St John Ambulance counties and I'm extremely honoured, as both friend and colleague, to take on the legacy that Ken leaves."

Ken was presented with gifts including a silver salver engraved with the St John Ambulance crest and a citation (pictured above).

Chesterfield Volunteer Ken Cook Receives Top Honour

Friday 7th October 2011

Ken Cook, a leading influence within St John Ambulance Derbyshire over the past decade, has been honoured with investiture as a Commander of the Order of St John - one of the highest honours which can be conferred on the charity's volunteers.

A former headteacher, Ken (left), of **Dronfield**, was a key member of the county team based in **Chesterfield**, taking on the top job as **Chair of Council** in 2007 and leading Derbyshire's 1,500 uniformed volunteers until he retired from the post last December.

He is now concentrating on other voluntary roles including **Deputy Lord Lieutenant, University of Derby governor** and **chair of Derby Family Nurse Partnership**, as well as working towards a doctorate in leadership and management.

Ken, who was already an **Officer of the Order of St John**, received his insignia at a special ceremony at the historic **Priory Church in London**.

Also honoured was **David Wright**, a former Chesterfield fire-fighter, who was invested as a **Member of the Order.** David, who recently moved to **Oxfordshire**, becamed the third generation of his family to join St John Ambulance when he signed up 37 years ago while working for **Coalite**.

The Order of St John is one of the world's oldest charities and traces its origins back 900 years to the **Knights Hospitaller** and the first **Hospital of St John in Jerusalem in 1078**. Membership of the Order is given only to those who have shown exceptional service. Each recipient is approved by the **Queen**.

CHAPTER 12

Celebrating the end of the Ambulance Appeal in Matlock,
July 2004

Cadet Leader Weekend,
March 2005

Princess Anne opens the extension of the
St. John Ambulance HQ. Chesterfield

Role reversal.
The St. John Ambulance summer camp

CHAPTER 12

Honoured by Her Majesty Queen Elizabeth as a Commander
of the British Empire (CBE) for services to education

loyalty and high professional standards. It was important to encourage both the staff and the pupils to be ambitious and to celebrate achievements, both academic and extracurricular. At this time, I was not familiar with the term 'glass ceiling' but I soon encountered the effect of teachers having low expectations and the impact on the lower achieving pupils. The school had a large special needs department. It didn't take long to realise that many of the pupils in this department were low achievers, not because of an inherent lack of ability but more as a result of their own low aspirations as a result of family background or lack of role models. The expectation of teachers could either confirm this or challenge it. What I found when I reviewed the practices of the staff in this department disturbed me but explained why many of the pupils had negative attitudes. It was clear that some of the teachers saw their role as being child minders with the sole aim of keeping difficult pupils occupied.

As I extended my reviews of the other departments I was pleasantly surprised at the quality of much of the teaching I observed. Many of the pupils were well motivated and most of the teachers were committed to helping the pupils to achieve high standards. The successful achievement of good 'O' levels and CSE results meant that the pupils were well qualified to enter the world of work or to continue with further post-16 studies, including 'A' levels. Unfortunately, the absence of sixth form provision was one of the reasons identified by parents as a cause of their rejection of the school as a destination for their children after primary school.

The opportunity to address this issue arose after the Sheffield Councillors made the decision to allow all secondary schools in the city to explore the possibility of offering post-16 courses. This was a political decision supported by the Labour politicians who needed to signal a commitment to equality. In the event, the decision proved easier than its implementation. Some senior Education Officers recognised the decision of the politicians was unsustainable and quickly set about trying to make the former secondary modern school commit to working cooperatively, preferably with one of the existing sixth form schools taking the lead. In the case of Rowlinson and Jordanthorpe, there appeared to be a strong justification. The two schools were geographically very close and there was a long history of pupils from Jordanthorpe transferring to post-16 studies at Rowlinson. There was only one problem. Many parents of the children in the Jordanthorpe catchment area were very clear about their wish for their children to attend an 11-18 school!

Together with the Head Teacher, I was invited to meet with some of the Education Officers and senior staff of Rowlinson at Rowlinson School. From the start of the meeting it became apparent that there had already been several meetings of this group at which decisions had been made. The purpose of this meeting was to inform us that Jordanthorpe should not start a sixth form. My Head Teacher had spent the last few years battling with the LEA, parents and some of the staff. I judged that she was approaching her final years in service and was seriously considering whether she wanted to embark on another conflict before her retirement. I was the young deputy with the prospect of a long career ahead contemplating both what the impact would be on my own career and that of the future status of the school.

However, after a brief consultation, we both decided that we should stand by our principles and address the issues of concern with the intention of making our school the one of choice in the area. We returned to the meeting to report our decision and received a series of dire warnings that there would be no support from the LEA and we were doomed to fail. On the other hand, we knew we had a supportive, powerful Governing Body with members who were prepared to roll up their sleeves to make our decision a success. Even so, the Governors recognised that by challenging the establishment we were embarking on an uncertain course of action. I remember a discussion with two of the Governors for whom I had the greatest respect. Bob Jackson, who later became the chair of the Governing Body, and Joe Bradley warned me of the personal risk of being seen to challenge the Authority. After their reassurances of support, we agreed to proceed. Bob and Joe obviously had faith in me. A year later, they were instrumental in my appointment as Head Teacher, despite resistance from some politicians and education officers.

After the meeting at Rowlinson, it was immediately urgent to start the process of changing the perceptions of the school. Engaging the staff and the pupils was not difficult, but winning over the parents needed something more dramatic. The parents identified the lack of sixth form as being a major impediment. The fact that the previously selective school were endowed with sixth form centres and were fully experienced in preparing students for 'A' levels made the provision of our own centre a priority. The refusal of the Local Authority to provide funding for additional accommodation to include a sixth form centre was expected. The door was not just closed, it was locked and bolted.

There had to be another way. Unexpectedly, a solution arrived. The local newspaper, 'The Star', reported that some prefabs that had been donated to Sheffield by the Tennessee Valley Authority at the end of the war were to be dismantled to make way for new permanent houses. I soon found somebody in the Works Department who agreed that we could have one of these prefabs as long as we took responsibility to remove it from the site. I immediately enlisted the support of two other members of staff and some members of our newly created sixth form and we spent two weekends dismantling the prefab and preparing it for moving to the school site.

Fortunately, my newly appointed chair of Governors, Bob Jackson, was not only the sports reporter on Radio Sheffield but his family business was based at the local vegetable market. The business owned a flat-backed lorry! Within no time the dismantled prefab was delivered and stored at the school. At this point, I should make it clear that I had no knowledge of building regulations and the need for planning consent. A visit from a Local Authority planning inspector was a revelation. I discovered that it was necessary to submit a full planning application with detailed drawings and evidence of compliance with the building regulations. Was this the end of the dream? After a sleepless night my brain kicked into action. The prefab came from America and there was, presumably, a possibility of locating the original plans. I immediately wrote to Washington explaining that the prefab had been donated to the people of Sheffield by the TVA and asked if they could help to locate a plan. To my astonishment, within a few days, I received a large envelope with American stamps. Enclosed was a copy of the building plan! I had great pleasure in telephoning the building inspector to inform him and then submitting the plan to the planning department. Several weeks later the department responded to the application. The notification said that the application could not be processed without proof that the proposal met the building standards regulations.

At this time, Joe Bradley, who was the head technician in the Physics Department at the University of Sheffield and vice chair of our Governing Body, came to the rescue. He knew someone who was a senior surveyor for a construction company in South Yorkshire who agreed to complete the necessary calculations, once again demonstrating the Yorkshire spirit that enjoyed supporting the underdog and challenging adversity.

At the beginning of the week prior to the October half-term break, I contacted the Building Inspector and invited him to come to school. He agreed and chose to visit on the following Friday because he was also scheduled to visit a road widening project close to the school that was not going to plan. I must confess to feeling rather smug as I anticipated the prospect of telling the inspector that I had successfully navigated every difficulty that I thought was preventing progress. It took about 10 minutes for my optimism to be dashed. The site we had chosen for the erection of the prefab was where a factory had once stood. The building had been demolished but the solid concrete foundation remained. In my naivety, I assumed that such a base would be perfect for a single-storey temporary building.

Strangely, the Inspector expressed genuine sympathy as he explained that the building needed a new foundation that, in his estimation, required a depth of about 4 feet to reach compacted clay. As he departed, he explained that there were also problems with the road widening project taking place outside the school.

As I contemplated what should happen next, I reflected on what I had learned about the Yorkshire and Sheffield spirit. The people took great pride in overcoming difficulties and proving their critics wrong. The thought of explaining to my Governors, staff and pupils that our project was about to fall at the final hurdle filled me with apprehension. It didn't take long for me to recall the conversation that I had with the Inspector when he told me about the problems encountered by the manager in charge of the road widening activity. There could have been a reason. Perhaps a conversation with the manager might prove useful. Later that day I decided to visit him. When I arrived at the site, he was sitting at a desk in a hut and he seemed happy to be interrupted. He was a young man and he listened attentively as I explained the importance of our project to those associated with the school. In response, he told me of a technical hitch that was preventing his workforce from getting on with their jobs. Eventually, he asked me what was the most urgent problem that we had encountered. I explained that it was the condition placed on us to provide a foundation by breaking the concrete base and digging a hole 30′ by 30′ about 4′ deep. He told me that his problem could not be solved immediately and, to my astonishment, he offered to send some men with diggers to excavate the foundations for the prefab. After I explained that we had limited financial resources, he said there would be no charge. I returned to school just as the pupils were leaving to enjoy a half-term break the following week, but I managed to catch the existing small group of sixth formers to explain that they would have to forego their holiday and be in school during the half term week. Agreement was unanimous. The beginning of the fightback was about to commence.

True to the promise of help to prepare the foundations the necessary heavy machinery arrived early on the Monday of half term. Within a few hours the work was completed but our good fortune didn't end there. Whilst the foundations were being prepared a brick layer from the Sheffield Council Works Department was carrying out some minor repairs on the school building. The bricklayer observed the action and soon enjoyed discussing the project with the 6th.formers. His name was Chris. Ford who, had apparently, recently built his own bungalow. With such expertise he was able to explain what actions were now needed. This included digging trenches around the bottom of the hole in order to create a suitable foundation for the construction of the walls that would support the building. The 6th.formers started this laborious task, but eventually, the road builders returned with the right equipment to finish it before the end of the day. By this time, Mr Ford was seen as part of our team. He was an older man but he clearly enjoyed the 'can do' spirit of the youngsters and he agreed that when the bricks for the supporting walls arrived, he would come to lay them. By the end of the half term week, the concrete foundations had been laid, and the bricks, cement, and sand had been delivered, ready for construction to begin. On the following Monday, there was a distinct change of atmosphere around the school. After the despondency created by the unfair criticism in the local press, there was a feeling of optimism which heralded a change from defence to offence. Negative articles in the newspapers were rigorously challenged.

As we moved into the positive phase of construction there were two issues that needed to be addressed. The overburden taken from the foundations was still lying around the hole. This was predominantly the remnants of the concrete base of the old factory. A brief discussion with the manager of the road project, together with a bottle of whiskey, resulted in an agreement that the lorries working on the road site would be loaded and the concrete removed. I understand that it was used as hardcore for a car park at a newly built local church. The second issue was about laying the bricks in the foundation of the prefab site. Mr Ford was already on board with this, and Alan O'Gram, the school caretaker, agreed to operate the cement mixer to provide the mortar.

With the foundation stage of the building now completed, it was now necessary to consider the skills we would need to finish the project. Joe Bradley, a man who was used to solving problems and blessed with immense skills, took charge of the final construction stage. I started to enlist the help of the parents, some of whom had specialist skills like electricians, plumbers, and joiners, but many others just wanted to be involved. Suddenly, the role of the school management changed from responding to antagonism to engaging the parents, pupils and staff in working together to achieve success. I am certain I could find academic references from the literature that would explain this transformation, but my observation of QPR identified that once the team members were all kicking in the same direction with desire and belief, then anything could become possible.

Over the next few years there were dramatic changes. Recruitment at Y7 and Y12 grew rapidly, the number of pupils progressing to university increased and the ethos of the school became more positive. However, further change was on the horizon. Miss Prebble decided she would retire at the end of the summer term. Whilst she was keen for me to apply for the headship, and the Governors supported this, there was little enthusiasm from the politicians and officers. Enshrined in the articles of governance for all secondary schools in Sheffield was the right of all governors to examine the applications of all candidates for posts at the school. There were two teacher and two pupil governors who, therefore, had the right to be involved in the shortlisting of candidates for interview. Their involvement would certainly have been to my advantage, but for some reason, the Officers and Teacher Unions agreed that none of these representatives should be involved.

On the morning of the interviews, together with the other candidates, I was invited to meet with the deputy director of Education, John Mann, at the Education Offices. I have a subjective view of this meeting, so I won't comment any further other than to say that I definitely felt that I was not the preferred candidate! The interviews were scheduled for the afternoon and at this level the panel was usually chaired by the Chairman of the Education Committee, Peter Horton. He was always viewed as a fair-minded pragmatist who would respect the quality of the interview and not start with a predetermined position. Sadly, on the day of the interview, he was in London attending a national meeting of Chairs of Education Committees, so a new chair, another Councillor, was appointed.

I have little memory of my actual interview except to say that I was aware that an Education Officer and a

City Councillor showed little tolerance for my clearly expressed view that, under the right leadership, the school had great potential. After all the candidates had been interviewed the panel took a long time to come to a decision, but eventually, I was invited back to the interview room to be offered the post. When most of the members of the panel had left, Bob Jackson and Joe Bradley came to my room to tell me that a local councillor had objected very strongly to my appointment and threatened to have the decision overturned at the next Council meeting. Apparently, he was very firmly informed by the substitute chair of the panel that the decision had been made and would not be changed. This person is no longer a Councillor, but he later had a high profile in South Yorkshire, performing an important role!

JORDANTHORPE SCHOOL
BUILDING A TEAM

The start of my new responsibilities as Head Teacher coincided with a period of industrial and teacher union unrest. At the national level, we had the oil crisis, which had a considerable impact on those schools that used oil to heat the boilers. There was also a problem with the reliability of public transport which meant that many of the teachers and pupils experienced difficulty in getting to school. At the same time, the Teacher Unions were reacting to the pronouncements of the Prime Minister, James Callaghan, about his concerns that education standards were not high enough and that schools were failing to prepare pupils for an increasingly complex world in which science, technology, and numeracy were critically important. The Teacher Unions chose to interpret the comments of the PM as an attempt to create a consensus around greater curriculum control, greater teacher accountability and the subordination of the purpose of secondary education to the perceived needs of an economy in crisis. This was not an ideal time to start my new responsibilities but the words of my recently deceased Dad entered my head. When faced with difficulties, he would often quote the words of Marshal Foch, a French military leader, in a message to his HQ before the battle of the Marne in the First World War:

My centre is giving way

My right is retreating

Situation excellent

I am attacking

My starting point was to address the disunity amongst the staff that had its roots in the amalgamation of the Boys' and Girls' Schools. My predecessor had been the Head Teacher of the Girls' School and the teachers who were previously at the Boys' School judged any of her decisions as prejudicial. Their complaints focused on the format of the timetable; the bias in internal promotions; favouritism in the allocation of departmental resources and the absence of support for staff in pupil disciplinary matters.

In previous years, the timetable was prepared by the Head Teacher with the help of an assistant head. It generally took several weeks to complete and it rarely involved consultation with the staff. As we approached the end of the term before I was to take up my appointment it was clear that the promised legacy of a prepared timetable was not going to happen. So, immediately after the spring bank holiday, I took control. At least I now had the opportunity to deal with an issue that the Heads of Departments identified as a serious concern. This was the policy of mixed-ability classes. For the following weeks, I remained at school late into the evenings, constructing a timetable that would meet the needs of each department. We were a 12-form entry school, so in years 7 to 9, I blocked classes in sets of 3 in English, mathematics, humanities, languages, science, etc. This allowed each department to decide whether to keep the mixed ability format or whether to set the pupils by ability. The Heads of Department were given the task of allocating the subject teachers to teaching groups. The construction of the timetable for years 10, 11 and 12 was slightly more problematic but once again this involved consultation with the Heads of Department, resulting in their ultimate ownership of the outcome.

The second complaint from the teachers involved bias in the selection of internal promotions. The Teacher Union Representatives indicated that this could become the subject of union action unless it was addressed. At first I thought it was a case of the Unions flexing their muscles until I started to investigate the matter. What I found concerned me greatly. There was no doubt that there was evidence of the allocation of posts of responsibility being more to do with whether your face fitted than pupil and departmental needs. Redistributing responsibility was not an issue that could be dealt with over night. My investigation uncovered the fact that most of the teachers were unaware of the distribution of responsibilities and that it was not the custom to advertise internal posts. There were so many reasons why this was wrong, so I drew up a proposal illustrating a fair distribution of responsibilities that would guide future promotions together with details of the existing situation. This provoked a number of interesting outcomes. In particular, it became apparent to the staff that there were some colleagues being rewarded with no accountability for, or expectation of, contribution to the success of the school.

I uncovered that a similar situation existed in the allocation of departmental funding. This was done by a private discussion between each head of department and the Head Teacher at the beginning of each financial year. I was not surprised by the result of my investigation of this matter. There were unexplained variations for which I could find no rationale. Once again, it was clear that greater transparency was needed with an agreed formula to decide the basic departmental allocations, together with an additional fund for necessary curriculum developments.

As my first term progressed, I began to detect a definite change in the atmosphere of the staff room. The disclosure of factual information, followed by development action plans, certainly challenged speculation and rumour. The teachers were developing a unity that focused on improving educational outcomes as well as creating extracurricular experiences and opportunities. However, whilst we had confronted some of the previously unfair criticism of the school and most parents were now pleased that their children were part of a newly invigorated institution there was still the legacy of concern about pupil behaviour. This was addressed by re-defining the role of the Heads of Year, each of whom had responsibility for 320 pupils and 12 form teachers. They now understood their role was one of leadership and not just maintenance. They recognised that their new priority was to encourage aspiration and achievement amongst their pupils, both in academic studies and in extra curricula opportunities such as sport, music, drama and community endeavours. Year assemblies would now allow public recognition of positive contributions. In addition, we started the annual pupil reviews at which I would meet with every pupil, together with their Head of Year and form teacher to acknowledge their achievements and agree targets.

From my point of view, I wanted to demonstrate to each one of my 1600 pupils that there was an obligation on them to be a credit to their school. Of course, there were some pupils whose behaviour did not meet expectations. So the question of sanctions needed to be addressed and remedial action plans clarified. Low-level misdemeanours were clearly in the province of the form teachers and heads of year, but for more serious misbehaviours, the pupils were referred to me. Often, a telling-off from the Head Teacher was enough, but sometimes, the involvement of parents became necessary. If this failed, a temporary exclusion or even a permanent expulsion would follow. Expulsion was seen as a failure, so we introduced a sanction before making such a decision. We had a supportive Governing Body and in appropriate cases the pupil and parents were invited to meet the disciplinary committee of 3 Governors who would consider the concerns about the pupil. Almost all the interviews ended with an agreement about future behaviour signed by the governor chair of the meeting, the Head Teacher, the parents and the pupil. Invariably, this succeeded in bringing about a change in behaviour.

I was a teacher for almost 40 years, mainly in schools that served deprived communities. Jordanthorpe did not quite fit into this category, but after the damage caused by the unfair and widely broadcast criticism by some members of the community and, indeed, by some members of the City Council, we had a mountain to climb. During my period as deputy head, we addressed concerns about the absence of the sixth form provision. The construction of the prefab had laid the seeds of a new, positive spirit amongst most parents and pupils. We had made great strides in putting aside former constraints by encouraging our pupils to challenge the 'glass ceiling' that previously prescribed their hopes and aspirations. As the first group of sixth formers left to take on new challenges, they were replaced by a growing number of new post-16 students who followed the pioneers to maintain the 'can do' spirit. However, the increasing size of the sixth form soon created accommodation problems. The new group embraced the earlier optimism and set about finding a similar building to the prefab. The following words from Helen Sharman, the first British Astronaut, illustrate the conditions the sixth formers had to endure but also demonstrates the power of determination and belief when young people are empowered to influence the future:

"The pre-fab was the epicentre of Jordanthorpe sixth form in the late 1970s. It was our place (I don't remember teaching staff ever going in there), somewhere we could go to be separate from the rest of the School and feel as though we were grown-up students; the building, along with not having to wear school uniform, was a significant part of our identity. I entered the sixth form in 1979, when the prevailing mood in the UK was fairly dismal, but our aspirations were pinned on the longer term with many of us not considering employment until after university or, at least, until after the sixth form period, which seemed like a long time in the future for us teenagers. However, I think the social climate contributed to our acceptance of basic prefab conditions as our 'space to be'. It was cold, condensation ran down the windows in the winter and as a non-smoker, I rarely ventured into the smoking room, which took up a good portion of the available space- it was the second largest of the three rooms, from memory. There was little to no desk area and I used to work on my knees while sitting on a plastic chair crammed next to friends doing the same, but our lessons were in the main school and free periods were few and far between. At least in the prefab, we felt free from imposed structure, free from teachers and parents, and free to make our own plans for the future."

— HELEN SHARMAN CMG OBE

Although we were entering a daunting period, the next 10 years proved to be the most exciting but challenging period of my career. There was a growing level of respect both amongst the teachers and between the teachers and pupils. There was also a developing culture of challenge when pupil behaviour fell below expected standards or their efforts in class were not acceptable. Teachers were also the subject of respectful challenge. The School Council became more active, rather than a token body, and earned the praise of a visiting HMI. The emphasis on opinions being based on fact was illustrated at one meeting attended by the HMI. On the agenda was an item to discuss dissections in biology classes. The pupil chair of the Council invited the Head of Department to attend the meeting to be held at the end of the day. I invited the HMI to join me at the meeting. The members of the Council fully understood that they were an advisory body and any policy decisions would involve the teachers, the Governing Body, the parents and the LEA. The Head of the Biology Department was asked to explain the justification for dissections in the main school biology curriculum. His cursory answer was challenged by members of the Council who had undertaken some thorough research to find that dissections were not a compulsory part of their course. At this point, the Head of Department agreed and the practice was ended. After the meeting, the HMI commented that the quality of the debate was excellent and mirrored a previous experience he had at a leading public school. He praised the teacher for his commitment to honest debate and for agreeing to change the practice.

This was not the only example of opinion eclipsing fact. One of our Governors was the Head Teacher of a feeder primary school that served a local, troubled housing estate. He would often claim that the majority of his pupils were destined to end up in our special needs department. It was almost said as a justification for poor performance, often resulting from mediocre expectations of his staff. By this time, we had several cohorts of sixth formers who had progressed through university. An analysis of the final class of degree that our former pupils achieved revealed that the majority of those who gained first-class honours degrees were former pupils of his school! Rather than focusing on achievable, aspirational targets, he preferred to justify mediocrity, which was not an option at Jordanthorpe.

During the early years of my headship, I was fortunate to have two very able deputies. One was Margaret Baranieski, who, despite her name, was a very straight-talking Scot and Dr David Moulson, a highly qualified physicist who had worked at Harwell before entering the teaching profession. We were a powerful team, and over 4 years, we worked together to ensure the delivery of a vision that enjoyed the support of all those associated with the school. Included in that vision was a determination to equip our pupils with the necessary skills to succeed as adults. We emphasised the value of the softer skills of reliability, respect and commitment for all pupils but, obviously, examination results and the achievement of the benchmark of 5 'O' levels or CSE grade 1's was used as the external judgement of success and something to celebrate. The school league tables emphasised the percentage of pupils at every school achieving this benchmark. I chose to focus on the actual number of pupils achieving it, which meant that each year I could report the actual number of additional pupils for whom the teachers had opened doors and, as a result, increased progression to either sixth form, FE College or an apprenticeship. However, the celebration of examination success was accompanied by a concern for those who did not achieve the benchmark. It would be easy to judge this outcome as success for some but failure for others. This was totally unacceptable to the teachers, but it was a dilemma faced by all schools. How could our school be made relevant to those who were unlikely to achieve the benchmark?

One of the lessons I had learned whilst teaching in my previous schools was that a lack of formal qualifications did not prevent the pupils from successfully undertaking difficult practical tasks. My trip to Hamelin, observing young soldiers carrying out the complicated task of building a bridge over the River Weser with great confidence was proof that there is a place for all talents regardless of the starting point. The outcome of this observation was that we organised a series of work experience placements where the measure of the pupil's success was how quickly they learned the new tasks, how reliable they were and how they related to their workmates. It was surprising how many were eventually offered permanent jobs at their work experience place when they left school at 16. Of course, the pupils still continued with studying when they were not on placement but many also enjoyed taking part in extracurricular activities. Every weekend and most evenings our sports teams were competing against other schools or at least remaining at the end of school, to practice. Similarly, the school orchestra, the choir and the drama group would be in evidence long after the end of school. The staff were creating opportunities that would lead to a lifelong interest for many pupils.

One teacher, in particular, gained national recognition for his projects involving engineering and computing. His name was Stan Spencer. After the oil crisis of the 1970s which resulted in the 3-day week and regular power cuts there was a growing commitment in the country for us to become less dependent on oil imports. In 1974, the Magnus Oil Field was discovered to the north of Shetland. There were major technical problems. Margaret Thatcher became the Prime Minister in 1979. There was considerable national interest in the project and the opening of the oil field was announced by the Prime Minister at a special ceremony in 1983. One of the technical problems was securing the stability of the drilling platform. It was not possible to anchor the platform to the sea bed, so a semi-submersible construction was devised. Stan encouraged a group of pupils to consider the problem and to construct a model to demonstrate the chosen solution to this technical difficulty. The group of pupils involved were invited to the official launch and enjoyed the opportunity to explain their model to Mrs Thatcher and the other dignitaries.

There were other projects as well. After a brief discussion with Stan, I told him of a holiday in Norfolk that I had taken with my family. I discussed the fact that my son had become very interested in Citizens Band Radio. Stan immediately saw an opportunity to connect our two buildings to encourage the pupils in the special needs department to expand their vocabularies. We didn't quite realise that you couldn't restrict outside contacts some of whom began to join the conversations. The custom was that participants on CB had names (handles) and the teacher of the special needs group chose the handle 'Country Lady'. We soon realised that she was attracting some undesirable contacts! Although we immediately ceased to use the CB facility, this had interested Stan in Amateur Radio. He soon established his World Communication Centre in a small cupboard and a number of senior pupils studied and achieved the qualifications of the amateur radio organisation.

A little later, Stan told me that some of the pupils would be attempting to contact the Challenger Space Craft. One of the spacemen was a radio operator and was willing to accept links whilst he was circling the Earth. As the spacecraft travelled over the UK, our pupils sent a message, hoping to make contact. Some weeks later, we received a communication from NASA confirming that contact had been made.

At a later date, the school had the opportunity to celebrate when a former pupil, Helen Sharman, became the first Briton in space!

Meadowhead School
Celebration

There is no doubt that the period up to 1986 was demanding but rewarding. After the difficulties that arose when the status of the school was changed from secondary modern to comprehensive there were substantial but successful changes. The sixth form was growing with large numbers progressing into higher education; examination results both at 16 and 18 were improving annually; the incorrect perceptions of bad pupil behaviour were challenged and there were now numerous expressions of satisfaction from parents. In addition, there was a high level of pupil involvement in many of the extracurricular opportunities. Our drama productions were acclaimed, our School orchestra was respected throughout the city and our sports teams were feared by their competitors. At the same time, residential experiences were offered, both at home and abroad.

However, a new cloud was to appear on the horizon. Until this time the FE Colleges that served the city were still under the control of the LEA. However, there was a proposal that colleges should become independent. This development appeared inevitable and there was certainly a sudden political will to make changes that would impact the schools. Eventually, the LEA proposed to amalgamate the colleges to form a single Sheffield College that would take control of all post-16 education and training. The new single college was to become the largest single provider of further education in the country. There was much speculation about the motive behind this decision. What was the purpose of this option when the outcome of either remaining the same or implementing the change would still result in independent FE provision. Many people suggested that political dogma determined the revisit to the previous decision about sixth form provision in the newly created comprehensive Schools. Some, of course, identified it as a result of the economic pressures that required a more extensively educated and trained workforce. Whatever the reason, there were serious changes ahead that would affect Jordanthorpe.

As time passed, the initial proposal was shaped, and an action plan evolved. Once again, there was a powerful body of opinion that wished to maintain sixth form provision in the former selective schools. These served the more affluent part of the city, and under pressure from the Conservative-led national Government, these schools were exempted from the proposal, although there was still a local political determination to proceed with the proposal for the remaining schools.

A key part of the adapted plan was to implement 3 amalgamations each of which involved 2 schools joining together. One of these amalgamations involved Jordanthorpe with a proposal to join with the adjacent Rowlinson to form the new Meadowhead School. The new school would be based on the former Jordanthorpe site thus permitting the Rowlinson buildings to become the Norton site of the Sheffield College.

Whilst the Sheffield Plan was evolving, there were other proposals from the central Government that would have an impact. As early as the 1960s there had been concerns expressed about teacher autonomy and the absence of accountability. It was the 'great debate' led by James Callaghan in 1976 that focused on the importance of the curriculum to deliver skills that would enhance the nation's economic prospects. The election of Margaret Thatcher in 1979 added impetus to the view that standards in schools would be raised by introducing an element of competition that empowered stakeholders to have access to concrete information about school performance. In 1988 this led to the Secretary of State for Education, Kenneth Baker, to introduce a National Curriculum, together with Local Financial Management. Now, the level of individual school funding became dependent on the level of pupil recruitment, which, it was believed, would be influenced by measures based on standard tests. Although it was a Labour Prime Minister who started this debate, it was seen by Sheffield politicians and others as a device by the Conservative Government to challenge local political control.

In their book' The Blunders of Our Governments' (2013), the authors King and Crewe explore the many decisions made by governments of either party that ended up with the exact opposite outcome to the intention. At the local level, Sheffield prided itself on being a city of the working class, and there is no doubt that the elected Labour Councillors believed that they were making decisions in the interest of the citizens. The creation of the single Sheffield College was seen as essential to empower more young people, who did not have the advantage of family example, to undertake further education or training. Did they judge that sixth forms were elitist? Who knows? But at the same time as the decision to create Sheffield College, there were two other, apparently unrelated decisions that questioned the perceived middle-class values. The first was the decision of the City Council to remove the power of

Governing Bodies to insist on pupils wearing school uniforms. This caused a series of bitter debates which culminated in a decision to allow the parents and pupils to vote on the matter. Over 95% of parents and 90% of pupils voted in favour of keeping uniforms! This caused problems for many City Councillors who had questioned the National Curriculum decision on the grounds of democratic principle but, despite the almost unanimous vote by parents and pupils, still imposed the ban on uniforms. The second decision was to second a large number of teachers (100+) for a whole year to attend one of the Sheffield Universities, hopefully, to consider and develop what became known as the 'Sheffield Curriculum' with assessments leading to new Sheffield-specific qualifications. This initiative was doomed to failure and certainly, as far as Meadowhead was concerned, it was unhelpful at a time of bringing together two Schools, each with a different culture. For many years each school had pursued practices that emphasised different priorities. The management and many of the staff at Rowlinson prided themselves on being at the forefront of new curriculum initiatives, whereas Jordanthorpe focused on stability. To bring about a successful amalgamation it would be necessary to have a clear strategy that would reassure parents and would give all teachers a vision of the future school that they could either support or choose to take one of the alternative options available. The LEA made it clear that the establishment would be created from the existing staff currently at each school. The problem was a combined excess number of teachers of 36 with the additional problem of excess support staff that had to be reduced.

Achieving this level of loss required the intervention of the LEA. The proposal was to offer three opportunities that all staff could consider. First of all there would be vacancies at the new FE College. Secondly, there would be the possibility for redeployment to other schools that might have vacancies and finally, there was a generous package of enhancement that might attract some teachers who were considering early retirement. There was one decision that, however, that the LEA chose to avoid making. Who was to become the Head Teacher of the newly created Meadowhead School? This matter could have caused difficulties. I met with the Head Teacher of Rowlinson on several occasions, and we made the joint decision that we would disagree in private, but we would always speak with one voice in public. In reality, the Head Teacher at Rowlinson was approaching retirement age and was already considering other options. This meant that the responsibility for devising and implementing a strategy fell on my shoulders. This burden was made more difficult because the assistant heads from both schools and several other senior staff decided that they would retire.

I spent the next few months consulting with teachers, support staff, parents and pupils in each school. The Jordanthorpe staff, with whom I had previously established an excellent relationship, expressed concerns that I no longer supported them, whereas the Rowlinson staff were concerned that I would impose alien demands for change that would challenge cherished projects. The parents identified that the clash of cultures would prevent any chance of a successful amalgamation, whilst the pupils felt there would be bloodshed as the former rivals clashed with each other. It was clear that only the removal of doubts about the future strategy for the new school would start the process of understanding and accommodation.

At this time, I think I must have been one of the very few head teachers in the country who welcomed the 1988 Education Act containing proposals for a national curriculum. At an early joint staff meeting, I was able to announce that this would be the guide and that the new structures would reflect the proposals in the Act. At the same meeting I was able to address a criticism that had become apparent from some of the unfamiliar staff. They expressed the view that they did not know what my beliefs were nor what my priorities would be to achieve them. My response was simple and in order to establish clarity, it was blunt. The task of teachers was to teach effectively and the responsibility of the pupils was to focus on learning. One of the characteristics of teachers that I have observed over years of practice is that they enjoy a good debate, but once their voice is heard, they focus on the task. It was a revelation to hear the conversations of teachers with different experiences discussing exactly what good teaching would entail. Almost certainly, the conclusion was that preparing our pupils for the next stage of their lives involved giving them some control over their own decisions. To make good decisions, the pupils needed to understand the consequences and that school performance would influence future opportunities. It was the duty of every teacher to encourage aspiration by demanding commitment.

Although it was going to take more than a year to complete the amalgamation and to bring Meadowhead School fully into existence, I was anxious to start implementing the decisions that were essential for success. The absence of commitment from several senior colleagues could have been an impediment but it turned out to be a blessing. Very soon, an interim Governing Body was appointed, some of whom I had worked with previously, but others who were political appointees, had a clear agenda. At the first meeting, I outlined my preferred structure and processes only to be challenged on my decision to use the National Curriculum format. Fortunately, 3 of the interim governors had served on the Jordanthorpe board and there were also 3 parent governors who expressed a wish for stability and certainty. It was reassuring to hear the 3 Jordanthorpe governors describing the problems faced several years earlier at the time when the school changed status and became a successful comprehensive school. The description of the immediate positive changes at the time and the following outcomes soon caused the Governing Body to endorse my proposals. After this approval the process of appointing staff to the new structure commenced. Ground rules about eligibility to apply for posts were agreed with the Teacher Unions. Where each school had similar posts of responsibility it was agreed that only those teachers would be eligible to apply. Fortunately, the school had similar middle management posts, such as heads of department and heads of year. When a choice had to be made between 2 candidates, one was appointed, and the other was offered an alternative responsibility on a protected salary. In fact many unsuccessful candidates chose to apply for a post either at the college or in another school. A few took the very generous early retirement option.

Eventually, all the sensitive staffing decisions were completed and we were able to consider how we should create unity amongst the pupils. During the term before the start of the new school, the staff worked tirelessly to create opportunities for joint activities. Arrangements were made for teaching groups, with pupils from both schools, to be established. At the same time there were joint sports teams, drama groups and music activities after school. This proved to be so successful that we were able to implement the new timetable two weeks before the end of term. This meant that on the first day of the return to school in September the pupils were familiar with their timetables, who their teachers would be and where they would be taught.

However, before the end of summer term, it was necessary to acknowledge the closure of 2 schools with a history of serving their communities. Each school planned closing ceremonies that respected their separate histories and achievements. At Jordanthorpe, we planned an event for which civic dignitaries, former staff members, and former pupils would be invited. It was planned that I would make the final speech. I must confess to spending much time in considering words that would respect the past but would positively anticipate the future. The day before the ceremony was sports day, and as I walked around the events, I was preoccupied with thinking about what I would say on the following day. The final events were the relays and the preparations were taking place around the track. At one staging point, a member of the PE staff was giving instructions to the participants. His words were relevant. "Take the baton and don't look back'" The theme of my final words at the closing ceremony were now obvious!

As the end of term would see the departure of all but one of the assistant heads it was important to advertise two posts for an appointment early in the new school year. There were internal candidates and I suspect that many of the staff would have assumed that two existing teachers, each of whom originated from one of the separate schools, would be appointed. It would have been an easy decision, and after the intensity of the year, it was a serious consideration. However, we were at the beginning of a new era and I recognised that every decision would be judged by old values. In the event, I recommended to Governors and the LEA that it would be best to appoint two new deputies who would not only bring fresh thinking but who could never be accused of favouring one of the former schools. The arrival of my new deputies emphasised a determination to make Meadowhead School an example of innovative practice accompanied by a demand for excellence. This was the first time that I was to be supported by two colleagues who were younger than me and who clearly had the potential to progress to greater things.

As the new relationship developed, I was able to delegate more responsibilities that would not only release me from day to day issue, but would give them the opportunity to develop the skills they would need to advance to headship.

After the introduction of local financial management I

observed that many of my fellow head teachers began to view their responsibilities more as a CEO with a focus on financial matters and human resources at the expense of the more traditional role of being a leading practitioner with a primary concern for educational outcomes. I had just been through a demanding period of change, and I realised that in order to achieve a successful amalgamation, my focus had been on management concerns rather than on the key role of effective teaching. The arrival of my two new colleagues, who welcomed the opportunity to take responsibility for day-to-day management issues, allowed me to reconnect with what should have been the primary purpose of all schools.

Fortunately, my two deputy heads proved to be highly competent in their new roles and this gave me the confidence to draw up a plan to spend three weeks with each department. The department reviews involving 12 – 15 teachers began with a full meeting with the staff at which the Head of Department would describe policies involving assessment, marking, lesson planning, achievement targets, resource allocation etc. After discussion involving the members of the department I explained my plan to visit lessons to assess whether the rhetoric was matched by the practice. At the end of 3 weeks, I delivered a report on my findings and discussed an action plan to correct any discrepancies. The benefit of this process was that the Head of

Department understood that their role was much greater than just being a good teacher and the teachers recognised their accountability in carrying out department practices.

Slowly, the issues that arose during amalgamation faded and the staff set about building a positive community in which everyone was valued and encouraged to achieve. However, early in 1997 the telephone call, feared by every school in the country, arrived. It was Ofsted informing us that there would be a full inspection within a couple of days. Although the staff recognised the importance of the relentless pursuit of good practice there was still a late night of activity to ensure that every possibility was covered. In the event, the feedback from the Inspectors was excellent and the school was judged as 'outstanding'.

When the report was published there was a great celebration by the staff, Governors, pupils, parents and the local community. Meadowhead, for a short period, was the first secondary school in Sheffield and, allegedly, South Yorkshire to achieve this accolade. The occasion was marked by a visit from the Secretary of State for Education, David Blunkett MP together with leaders from the Sheffield Council. It was, indeed, a considerable achievement.

Sheffield LEA
14-19 Agenda

It didn't take long for the euphoria after the inspection to calm down. Very soon, we were back on course, striving to show we were worthy of our newfound recognition. There was one thing, though, that was certainly different. My relationship with politicians and officers became much more cordial. The appointment of a new Director of Education, Jonathan Crossley-Holland, was instrumental in bringing about this change. Soon after the Ofsted inspection, Jonathan visited the school. As both of our buildings were in need of a complete refurbishment, I took the opportunity to take him on a tour of the sites. I was anxious for him to meet staff and pupils and to view the poor conditions in which they worked. During the course of the tour I realised that there was another reason for his visit when he asked me if I would like to be seconded to the LEA as an advisory head teacher with responsibility for the 14-19 agenda. I must confess that after the inspection, I had considered whether it was time to move on and to make way for a younger person who would ensure that the school continued to improve. These thoughts controlled my response to the Director. I thought a secondment would leave the school in limbo so I decided to take retirement and to work for 3 days a week from the Education Offices and to take consultancy opportunities with Nord Anglia.

The Director had realised that a characteristic of secondary head teachers was that they would not give credence to advice from anyone who had no experience of the complexity of headship. I fitted the bill, and I started the task of trying to develop a single 14-19 agenda, which involved the schools with sixth forms, Sheffield College and other training providers. I met regularly with the head teachers to discuss sacrificing some autonomy for the greater good. This would challenge the strict entry requirements that were needed to be allowed to embark on 'A' level courses in the sixth forms. It was also obvious that, other than in exceptional cases, preference would be given to those pupils who had attended the same school for their pre-16 education. The consequence of this was that many of the pupils attending the 11-16 schools were denied a sixth form opportunity and were left with the options of attending the Sheffield College, taking an apprenticeship, seeking unskilled employment or unemployment.

My meetings with the College and training providers were more productive. In comparison to the sixth form schools, which were only willing to enrol pupils who were almost certain to succeed, the College and Training Providers were anxious to offer opportunities that could lead to both educational and vocational qualifications. The measurement of their success was not just based on results but on the opportunities they were able to offer, whereas the schools were only judged on successful pupil performance in external assessments.

For most of my career, I shared the concerns of the head teachers, but after amalgamation and before Ofsted, I began to take a wider interest in city affairs, which led me to examine my own priorities. Until this time, like most head teachers, I was anxious for my school to perform well in the league tables that were based on test and examination results. It was not until much later that account was taken of more sophisticated calculations such as value added. As a result of my appointment as the Advisory Head Teacher, I developed a wider profile in the city. I became Chairman of the Education and Business Partnership; I served on the Strategic Education Forum, chaired by the Master Cutler, and I was appointed to be a member of the Training and

Enterprise Council, later to become the Learning and Skills Council for South Yorkshire. In addition, I was asked to join the Governing Body at Sheffield Hallam University. Suddenly, my previous rather parochial focus on my school was challenged by a concern about opportunities for all Sheffield pupils and a realisation that league tables led to competition between schools, which meant that some were seen as successful whilst others were viewed as failing. I would like to claim that my efforts to bring about a unified policy for 14-19 education and training was a success, but this aspiration was blunted by the intransigence of some of the constituents.

As this realisation was dawning on me, I was asked to meet with the Director of Education. For some time, he had been wrestling with the problem of poor performance by some secondary schools. One, in particular, was Earl Marshal School, which was based in the industrial north of the city. The school was one of the 18 'named and shamed' identified nationally. At this time, the Secretary of State for Education was David Blunkett MP. Earl Marshal served a predominantly Muslim community that overlapped with his constituency. The Director informed me that, despite the initiation of a 'fresh start' process, the school had failed to attract a suitable candidate to be the Head Teacher. The only solution was to make a temporary appointment of an experienced head teacher. After I agreed that this would be wise, he informed me that the experienced head teacher was me!

EARL MARSHAL/FIR VALE SCHOOL
FRESH START

Earl Marshal School was located in the area of Fir Vale to the north Sheffield. This is a disadvantaged area with an ethnically diverse population of Pakistani, Somali, Yemini and Caribbean origins, together with a minority of older indigenous residents. The pupil roll at the school reflected this mix. The need to appoint a new head teacher in 1990 led to the bold decision to appoint Chris Searle, who was an anti-racist, socialist activist with an unusual background. Chris had been a teacher at the John Cass Foundation School in the east end of London. He was dismissed from his post for publishing a collection of poems written by his pupils contrary to the instructions of his head teacher. He was later re-instated after his pupils decided to strike in his support. Eventually, his deeply held beliefs led him to continue his teaching career in Mozambique and the Caribbean where , he believed, his socialist and anti-racist principles would be appreciated. In the late 1980s he decided to return to the UK at a time of change in education policies both at the national and local levels. At this time, the Sheffield Council was led by a group of intellectual socialists who objected to the new education policies outlined in the 1988 Education Reform Act, which was supported by the Conservative Government led by Mrs Thatcher. However, in one area, the local politicians were not in conflict with national priorities, and one decision received support at all levels. This was the importance of addressing the issue of multiculturalism. In accord with the changing character of the city, Sheffield Councillors made the decision to advertise for an adviser for Multi-cultural Education. It was still a surprise, however, when Chris Searle was appointed to the post. He certainly had the experience of teaching in different communities and he, therefore, had the credibility that warranted the risk of his appointment. Perhaps the deciding factor was his interest in cricket, a game that crossed all barriers of race, nationality, class, gender and inclusion!

In 1990, Chris was able to further his commitment to multi-cultural education by being appointed as the Head Teacher of Earl Marshal School. Despite his lack of experience in school management he had the support of the Councillors, many of whom were active in pursuing the vision of a Socialist Republic of South Yorkshire.

During his 5 years as Head of Earl Marshal I would meet him at regular gatherings of the Sheffield Secondary Heads Group. On several occasions, I gave him a lift back to his school, and I enjoyed discussing his philosophy, which he eloquently explained. One key pillar of his thinking was his non-exclusion policy. The problem was that he did not gain the support of the teachers who found the behaviour of some pupils so challenging to the point of total disruption in the classrooms. Inevitably, the teachers were opposed to the continuation of this policy and they attempted to derail it. This resulted in a BBC Panorama programme which involved some of the teachers in expressing an outright condemnation of his leadership and the school ethos. Eventually, after an Ofsted inspection where there was criticism of lack of standards, poor pupil behaviour and ineffective management the School was placed into special measures. Chris Searle eventually resigned; this was followed by the appointments of a temporary and later permanent head teacher, both of whom failed to garner the support of the community and of the teachers. It was at this point that I became involved as a representative of the LEA to serve on the Governing Body. By this time, the Director of Education had already made the decision to take the school through the 'fresh start' process, which involved closure and reopening as a new school with a new head teacher and teaching staff.

It was a difficult time. The Teacher Unions were unhappy that the existing teachers would not automatically transfer to the new school. After a lengthy debate and consultation with the DFE about the 'transfer of undertakings' regulations, it was agreed that the existing staff would be given priority rights to an interview and that each appointment would be competitive and open to external candidates. The recently appointed unsuccessful Head was made redundant with the granting of immediate 'gardening leave' and the procedure leading to the appointment of a new Head Teacher for the now proposed renamed Fir Vale School started immediately. When the post was advertised, there was a poor response, as a result of which, it was decided not to proceed with the appointment. It was at this point that the Director of Education asked me to take the temporary post of Head Teacher and to immediately start the process of appointing the new staff in order to be ready for a new beginning as Fir Vale in the following September.

This began a period of hectic activity of preparing for the new school whilst attempting to impose reasonable standards of behaviour amongst the pupils and ensuring that the teachers, most of whom would not be part of the new school, were carrying out their professional responsibilities at an acceptable standard. In addition, there were external community issues involving rivalries between adults from different national groups that frequently erupted into violent clashes outside of the school.

The realisation that my reputation as a Head Teacher for 22 years at a school that had only recently been judged as 'outstanding' paled into insignificance as I realised that only the next 18 months would decide my legacy. Fortunately, my involvement with wider Sheffield activities gave me access to some influential people who genuinely wanted to contribute to the success of the school. Several of these people agreed to join the Governing Body. It wasn't all good, however. There was some discussion amongst cynical people about the vast salary I would be receiving. For the sake of the record, I refused to take the full salary and only accepted an amount that represented the difference between my teacher's pension and the salary I would have been receiving at Meadowhead. It comforts me to know that those colleagues I have worked with and know me well would vouch for my integrity. I didn't choose to be a teacher for monetary rewards. I became a teacher to make a difference and to improve the life chances of those I taught.

The period leading up to the end of the summer term was very busy. I was determined that the new school would seamlessly convene in the following September with a full complement of staff and a balanced budget. I was delighted with the quality of the candidates who we called for interview and appreciated the unanimous understanding of the successful appointees that it would be difficult for them to meet as a group until after the end of term when the old staff had left. Fortunately, most of the unsuccessful staff were offered redeployment or early retirement.

At the same time, when dealing with staffing issues, there were other groups to be consulted. The Governors, of course, were familiar with the planning and several took part in the interview process. However, predictably, the pupils, parents and community would play a critical part in deciding the success, or otherwise, of the Fresh Start initiative. I was surprised when I learned that it was not the custom at Earl Marshal to hold whole school assemblies. Throughout my career, I had learned to appreciate the value of formal gatherings where expectations can be expressed, praise given, and respect demonstrated. The old staff had reported that there was concern at Earl Marshal that large gatherings would lead to opportunities to challenge the authority of the staff. This had to be challenged and the policy of the new Fir Vale School was that there would be whole school daily assemblies. For most schools, this is the usual practice at the start of the day. At Fir Vale, it was a clear assertion that the teachers were now in charge and that the assemblies would have a spiritual dimension by the delivery of a thought for the day followed by praise for positive events and condemnation of any actions by individuals that brought criticism on the school and the pupils. The focus was almost certainly about choices and consequences. As we embedded new standards and expectations, Fir Vale was no longer an experiment. It was a normal school emphasising the pursuit of ambitious achievement with an expectation of respect for each other and for those tasked with the preparation of the pupils for their future lives.

As the year progressed the parents and the wider community started to become more involved in supporting the school. The teachers also became more active in helping the community to address the racial issues that occasionally erupted into conflicts between different national groups. I certainly became aware of the important role the school could play in bringing about greater community cohesion at a time when anti-racist rhetoric emphasised the protection of differences rather than the benefits of unity.

As my task at Fir Vale approached completion and a new substantive Head Teacher was appointed, it gave me great pleasure to look back on a job well done. The school was now stable and focused on priorities that were certainly valued by all associated with the school. As I handed over the reins to my successor, I had every confidence in a successful future for Fir Vale and I looked forward to a peaceful retirement.

However, once again, events intervened. I had worked

closely with Mo Laycock, a fellow Head Teacher of the adjacent Firth Park School. Mo had worked tirelessly to establish leadership support for school leaders across South Yorkshire. Together with Professor Di Bentley at Sheffield Hallam University, they developed the idea of setting up a Leadership Centre at the university that would deliver training for senior school staff throughout the region. I think they saw an opportunity to implement their plan and they asked me to accept the role of Director with the task of setting up the centre. I took this offer as a compliment that I could not refuse, so my plans for a quiet life in my garden were put on hold!

THE SOUTH YORKSHIRE
LEADERSHIP CENTRE

I started my career as a teacher in secondary modern school serving pupils from a deprived community and later as a Head Teacher for 22 years at one of the largest comprehensive schools in Sheffield and South Yorkshire that was recognised by Ofsted as 'outstanding'. I finished as the interim Head Teacher of a school that served a predominantly mixed immigrant area of North Sheffield. My accounts of the changing demands placed on these schools and the teachers demonstrate that this was a period of transition that demanded greater skill of those tasked with the management responsibilities of these changes.

At the time, I was a Governor at Sheffield Hallam University, and I was fully conversant with the work of the staff of the School of Education to develop suitable training courses that focused on the enhanced management skills required by those who were to manage our schools. However, as I approached the completion of my task at Fir Vale, there was a growing concern that the focus on transactional management skills was not enough in preparation for the unpredictable changes ahead. This led to the university and the Directors of Education for the South Yorkshire Authorities to identify the need for a new breed of school leaders who could embrace transformational changes.

Professor Di Bentley, the Head of the School of Education at Sheffield Hallam, together with Mo Laycock, the Head Teacher of Firth Park School in Sheffield, led the debate on the best way to achieve this. Their decision was to propose the setting up of the South Yorkshire Leadership Centre based at the university but serving the schools in the 4 local authorities. The decision to proceed with the establishment of the centre, either by chance or design, coincided with the completion of my work at Fir Vale, and I was asked to take on the role of Director with an office provided by the university but no funding for courses or external experts. It was my task to establish a Centre that would encourage education leaders throughout South Yorkshire to embrace a culture of lifelong learning and continuing professional development. The centre eventually worked in partnership with the four LEAs (Barnsley, Rotherham, Doncaster and Sheffield), Sheffield Hallam University and the Dearne Valley Business School at Doncaster College. By encouraging close partnership, the centre acted as a catalyst for change in the region by ensuring that head teachers and other leaders within schools, colleges, higher education and the wider community understood the importance of their role in contributing to the economic strategy for the region by supporting initiatives that would improve the educational attainment of young people, thus contributing to regeneration.

The changes in the fortunes of Fir Vale had earned the School considerable news coverage in the local newspaper and Radio Sheffield. Because of this I had a positive response from the Regional Development Agency to a request for funding. This was granted, and the centre received an allocation of nearly £400000.00, which was gratefully accepted. At the same time, I met Andre Haynes, who was employed by Lloyds TSB to deliver training using the European Foundation for Quality Management (EFQM) model. He agreed to deliver a series of training sessions in each of the 4 Teachers' Centres to introduce senior teaching staff to the model. The support of Andre and Lloyds TSB at this time proved to be invaluable. Many senior staff throughout the region were seeking guidance on how to improve their management skills, and the immediate implementation of training courses raised the profile of the newly created South Yorkshire Leadership Centre within each Authority.

However, whilst the school leaders and potential leaders viewed the Leadership Centre as a valuable source of support and training, it was more difficult to engage with some of the education officers. It was also important to raise the profile of the School of Education at Sheffield Hallam University as an essential partner. The development of the concept of the Leadership Centre owed a great deal to the Professor of Education, Di Bentley, who encouraged the Vice Chancellor, Professor Diana Green to host an official opening of the centre to be carried out by David Blunkett MP who, at this time, was the Secretary of State for Education. At the launch, we arranged a video address from Professor Andy Hargreaves who was based at the University of Ottawa in Canada. He was the leading expert on transformational leadership and the fact that we were able to receive his contribution from the other side of the Atlantic made me realise that the Leadership Centre and the university could link more easily with leaders throughout our region. So, in time, we used a substantial amount of the grant from the Regional Development Agency to install video conferencing facilities in each Teacher Centre and at the university, thus creating a facility for training sessions to be delivered simultaneously throughout the South Yorkshire region by the School of Education lecturers. Eventually, the work of the Leadership Centre was absorbed into the School of Education.

REFLECTIONS

Throughout our lifetimes all of us are faced with making decisions. Many of these decisions are inconsequential but others are life defining, the consequence of which will stay with us forever. In this book I have tried to address the two key choices that I made as a young man that have provided stability and have guided me through those periods of turbulence and doubt.

The first decision was to become a teacher. It was not to embark on a safe career, as my Dad advised, that would lead eventually to a secure pension in my old age. It was my desire to share the spirit of rebellion and independence that my own teachers had encouraged in me and my classmates. I wanted to help young people to overcome barriers and challenge conformity when the system said 'it can't be done'.

My second decision was to come to Sheffield, an industrial city with a worldwide reputation for quality craftsmanship and innovation with a population that enjoyed a community spirit that encompassed immense pride in its history and an unwavering optimism about the future.

As soon as I started teaching at Coleridge Road Secondary Modern Boys' School and later at Park House, I became aware that the pupils had a priority of loyalties. The first was the support of a football team which was either Wednesday or United. The second was the belief that Yorkshire was the best county at cricket, and the third was that their school and teachers were the best in the city. At this time, the purpose of school was clearly defined and understood. Whilst all schools shared a commitment to the 3 key pillars that defined their purpose, each school was able to give priority to the specific needs of their pupils. Some, particularly the selective schools, emphasised the achievement of high academic standards, whilst others saw their main role as the development of character and the encouragement of cultural values.

THE PURPOSE OF SCHOOL

KNOWLEDGE

- Intellectual development
- Subject mastery
- Academic study/critical thinking
- Problem solving/practical skills
- Preparation for work

CULTURE

- Equality and social Justice
- Democracy
- Moral Purpose
- Compromise and collaboration
- Teamwork
- Diversity
- National Values/history

CHARACTER

- Emotional Intelligence
- Resilience
- Curiosity
- Self-confidence
- Challenge
- Critical thinking
- Persistence

After a period spanning many decades, during which the procedure for the delivery of learning was not questioned, the 1970s saw a transformation of our national priorities to address the apparent failure of schools to contribute to our national economic success. The wider purpose of schooling, which included cultural, democratic and social goals, was subordinated in the national drive to rise up the International PISA performance league tables. This change of emphasis not only led to consideration about the fundamental purpose of schooling but also the quality of the preparedness of newly qualified teachers to deal with the changing demands. When I trained to be a teacher, the key measure of success for a newly qualified entrant to the profession was about classroom control and discipline. Today a new entrant is still faced with this expectation but, in addition, a greater imperative is to improve the academic performance of the pupils. At the same time, recent changes in the population structure of our society, with greater ethnic mix, require an appreciation and sensitivity about diversity and the previous focus on character development, which was often interpreted as a 'stiff upper lip', requires teachers to consider wellbeing, emotional intelligence and respect for those with differing needs and values.

In the current climate, it would be understandable for teachers to focus only on preparing pupils for external assessments. It is often these measures that parents and others use to judge the quality of a school. However, whilst the achievement of academic benchmarks is often critical in deciding future career opportunities and life chances, it is not the only quality that will help pupils to achieve fulfilment in their adult lives. Over many years as a teacher I realised that most pupils who were not destined to achieve outstanding academic success had other qualities that gave them opportunities to develop leadership skills, resilience and self confidence. These opportunities were often made available by committed teachers who organised extracurricular activities involving sports, music, drama, and other clubs that made school relevant and allowed the pupils to recognise and explore other talents that gave them status.

In recent years I have become concerned by the pressure on teachers to demonstrate a commitment to the achievement of measurable targets that focus on test and examination results. It is understandable that other activities are considered as less important. However, current national concerns about the character of many young people and the apparent lack of moral purpose indicate a need to explore ways to create acceptable opportunities for cultural and character development. Our limited success in rising higher in the PISA tables could be judged to have been achieved at the expense of the other values of tolerance and respect for those pupils who were either not academically gifted or, for whatever reason, lacked motivation. The national emphasis on higher academic standards may impede opportunities for schools to encourage activities that might lead to greater community cohesion. Whilst it is indisputable that our schools have a clear responsibility to prepare our young people to be able to contribute to our national economic performance, there is also a need to ensure that pupils receive guidance and example that values those other qualities that create good citizens. The difficult question is, of course, whether this should be the sole responsibility of already overworked teachers.

When I retired, I was appointed to a voluntary role as the Commander of Derbyshire St. John Ambulance. My responsibilities encompassed the work and training of our volunteers, including the cadets, and the business side of the organisation which earned an income to pay the salaries of our trainers and clerical support. I soon appreciated the commitment of volunteers to undertake training to become qualified first aiders or ambulance technicians. Few of our volunteers would claim to have been outstanding school students, but all completed training at an appropriate level that allowed them to contribute to their communities. I was so impressed by the commitment and social conscience of many that, in co-operation with the University of Derby, we developed a foundation degree in voluntary sector leadership and management which acknowledged the

St. John qualifications but also created other units of study, the successful completion of which would contribute to the award of a foundation degree. Those volunteers that gained this qualification not only enjoyed recognition that granted status amongst their colleagues, but it also opened wider opportunities and recognition in their employment. St. John has a large contingent of cadets who are well trained in leadership skills with an expectation of success which would benefit all young people. There are many other youth organisations with similar standards. Could there be an opportunity to deliver the 3 pillars of purpose by creating a more formal relationship between our schools and the voluntary sector?

About the Author
KEN COOK CBE DL

Ken came to Sheffield in 1961, where he enjoyed a successful career as a teacher in the industrial east end of the city and later as the Head Teacher, for 22 years, of one of the largest secondary schools in Sheffield, which he transformed from being a 'bog standard' comprehensive, heavily criticised by parents and the community, to gaining the Ofsted accolade as 'outstanding'.

After retirement, he returned to active service when he was asked to lead one of the 'named and shamed' failing schools through the 'fresh start' process. The success of this venture, together with his previous exemplary career record, earned him the reputation as being a 'super head' and national recognition when he received a CBE for services to education.

Throughout his career, Ken has demonstrated his belief that schools should encourage pupils to develop the personal qualities of reliability, persistence and respect and to have the confidence to take risks and to challenge injustice.